Enlightenment
NOW

"Jason Gregory takes to heart the famous slogan of twelfth-century Tantric Buddhist master Chekawa Yeshe Dorje when he writes 'Self-liberate even the antidote.' The message is that in the end, even our zealous, pious practice of spiritual disciplines need to be left at the door to step into the timeless bliss of full awakening, of enlightenment. Though such practices are considered by aspirants to be more effective and/or valuable than the awakening that life itself offers us in each moment, few are willing to break the shackles of display of sacred appearance, to live in each moment—awaken to a sneeze, the movement of waves, the giggle of a baby—free of any religious mantle. Read and savor *Enlightenment Now* as a celebration of our true and timeless nature."

ROBERT SACHS, AUTHOR OF *BECOMING BUDDHA,*
THE PASSIONATE BUDDHA, AND *THE ECOLOGY OF ONENESS*

"Jason Gregory takes us on a spiritual journey deep into the dark world of polarized perception, showing how suffering and veiled consciousness developed. Then he leads us right back out again. We end up returning to where we've always been, and we get the cosmic joke! As usual, he integrates many fine points into an interesting and comprehensive narrative."

PENNEY PEIRCE, AUTHOR OF
LEAP OF PERCEPTION AND *FREQUENCY*

"An erudite and scholarly overview of our spiritual struggle to arrive at a place where, ironically, we already are. Quoting amply from many literary references, this multilayered book documents man's historic spiritual quest for the very core of Truth. By fully addressing the paradox of awakening, the author points out that enlightenment itself is nothing other than the discovery of our very own true nature. If you're willing to take the time to carefully read this intelligent and in-depth exposé, there are many hidden treasures to be mined here. Recommended."

CHUCK HILLIG, AUTHOR OF *ENLIGHTENMENT FOR BEGINNERS*

"Jason Gregory has done it again. With a deep understanding of spiritual, psychological, and linguistic traditions he reveals how we are hypnotized into a disconnected worldview. This latest book strips away the veneer from our fast-food culture of consumerist enlightenment and points toward the need for genuine individual self-work. Gregory shines clarity onto the false joyride of our lives and makes us see clearly that the journey itself is the destination. *Enlightenment Now* is the ideal antidote to the spiritual sloth endemic in our 'get quick' cultures. Highly recommended!"

KINGSLEY L. DENNIS, AUTHOR OF *THE PHOENIX GENERATION*
AND *NEW CONSCIOUSNESS FOR A NEW WORLD*

"In *Enlightenment Now,* Jason Gregory has provided a comprehensive overview of man's search for enlightenment. His research draws upon a wide range of resources and walks the reader through perspectives of modern philosophy and culture all the way back to the ancients. One nice feature is that the book is rich with wisdom quotes from sages. Along the way, Jason includes his own commentary and suggestions for the contemporary seeker as to what works, what doesn't, and why. It is a book many readers will benefit from and enjoy."

PETER DZIUBAN, AUTHOR OF
CONSCIOUSNESS IS ALL AND *SIMPLY NOTICE*

"Jason Gregory has done a fantastic job of cutting through to the heart of enlightenment and the spiritual teachings of the ancient wisdom traditions. The illusory nature of the spiritual journey is explored with a profound clarity that will certainly help to guide those interested in meditation and personal liberation."

DAMO MITCHELL, AUTHOR OF
DAOIST NEI GONG

"This book reminds us that enlightenment is nowhere else to be found other than within the confines of our own skin. He eloquently describes how easy it is to lose sight of our own capabilities, living in a world that is too often governed by greed and profit. Jason's simple yet effective solution is to live in the moment and thereby find the answers we seek within."

GARY WAGMAN, PH.D., L.AC., AUTHOR OF
YOUR YIN YANG BODY TYPE AND
FOUNDER OF THE AMERICAN INSTITUTE
OF KOREAN TRADITIONAL MEDICINE

"A philosopher's view regarding the endless paradoxes we encounter on our way to enlightenment—Jason rightly points out that enlightenment is not something we can attain like a new car; for ultimately, enlightenment is 'no thing.' Yet, it is a 'no thing' that we can realize, that brings ultimate freedom. But here again there is paradox, for the freedom of enlightenment is not free; it entails discipline of body, mind, and speech. It does free us from the jail of our conditioned habits and egocentric behaviors, but at the cost of realizing that every action we take is ultimately beyond our personal control, interdependent upon the movement of the entire universe. As a philosopher, I revel in Jason's correction of our mistaken views regarding enlightenment."

RICHARD MILLER, PH.D.,
DEVELOPER OF IREST MEDITATION AND AUTHOR OF
YOGA NIDRA: THE MEDITATIVE HEART OF YOGA

"At times I am weary of individuals using, with their own uniqueness, terms and images from a long established tradition. However, when I read Jason's work it becomes evident that he himself does not attach to these terms and images. Instead he seems to show that some universal intelligence has always been present with humanity and our universe. I love his message because I feel it with all the reverence of my heart. There is nothing to strive for that isn't already in the room with us right now. Right off the bat, the first chapter nails this point with the most modest of hammers. His words are still ringing within me. Good job yet again, Jason."

BEN STEWART, DOCUMENTARY FILMMAKER OF
KYMATICA AND *UNGRIP*

ENLIGHTENMENT NOW

Liberation Is Your True Nature

JASON GREGORY

Inner Traditions
Rochester, Vermont • Toronto, Canada

Inner Traditions
One Park Street
Rochester, Vermont 05767
www.InnerTraditions.com

Text stock is SFI certified

Library of Congress Cataloging-in-Publication Data

Names: Gregory, Jason, 1980– author.
Title: Enlightenment now : liberation is your true nature / Jason Gregory.
Description: Rochester, Vermont : Inner Traditions, 2016. | Includes
  bibliographical references and index.
Identifiers: LCCN 2016009617 (print) | LCCN 2016035380 (e-book) |
  ISBN 9781620555910 (pbk.) | ISBN 9781620555927 (e-book)
Subjects: LCSH: Liberty—Religious aspects. | Spirituality. | Spiritual life.
Classification: LCC BL65.L52 G74 2016 (print) | LCC BL65.L52 (e-book) |
  DDC 204/.2—dc23
LC record available at https://lccn.loc.gov/2016009617

Printed and bound in the United States by Lake Book Manufacturing, Inc. The text stock is SFI certified. The Sustainable Forestry Initiative® program promotes sustainable forest management.

10 9 8 7 6 5 4 3 2 1

Text design by Virginia Scott Bowman and layout by Priscilla Baker
This book was typeset in Garamond Premier Pro and Minion Pro with Avenir used as a display typeface

To send correspondence to the author of this book, mail a first-class letter to the author c/o Inner Traditions • Bear & Company, One Park Street, Rochester, VT 05767, and we will forward the communication, or contact the author directly at **jasongregory.org**.

Contents

Acknowledgments

ENLIGHTENMENT NOW was a book gestating within me for many years. It was the result of many years of travel, hundreds of books I've read, meeting many teachers and students of numerous wisdom traditions, and my own willingness to go into isolation to explore the ancient traditions and their spiritual practices, which I now know is timeless wisdom that has more significance now than ever before considering the speed of the world. The outcome of all this is a synthesis of many wisdom traditions, especially from the East, to explain and clarify for the modern world the core wisdom of many ancient spiritual philosophies resulting in the basis and heart of this book. For this book to be what it is requires a lot of effort and dedication on my part, but also a lot of support from many people who all contributed to it in many different ways. None more so than the following people I will mention.

I am extremely grateful to the whole team at Inner Traditions and Bear & Company, not only for their care and support of my own work, but also for producing quality content consistently for many years. I am especially thankful to Jon Graham for believing in my work, supporting my books, and for recommending this one for publication. Thank you also to Ehud Sperling, the mind behind Inner Traditions, for seeing the depth of this book and its need to be out there in the world. To both of my editors, I am in awe at the detailed work both of you achieved for this book. First of all to my copyeditor, Ben Gleason, thank you for pinpointing key areas of the book that needed more clarification and also for challenging me in parts of the book, which allowed more of the text to come forth and shine. Secondly, to my project editor, Meghan MacLean, a heartfelt thank-you for your care, guidance, and wisdom during the editing process. Thank you for putting up with me again and having the warmth to deal with any obstacle we met.

Special gratitude goes to all the wonderful people of Chiang Mai in Thailand, especially the Saraphi district just outside of the city where this book was written, in a somewhat isolated environment. All of the beautiful smiles, kind hearts, and awesome food were the only fuel I needed to stay focused and motivated to write this book.

Most of all, loving gratitude to Gayoung, my beloved wife and spiritual companion. Thank you for having the strength and commitment to live an adventurous life with me. And though it may be an unconventional and uncertain life at times, we both know it is a real life that fulfills both our hearts. Your kind patience and understanding when I am in the tornado of my writing process is something we can all learn from. I know I certainly have.

Out of Time and Into Enlightenment

THE MOST IMPORTANT MYSTERY that we encounter on our endeavor to be free in this life is that what we seek we already possess. This statement not only goes beyond the psychological parameters of what we believe freedom to be in this life, but it also destroys the concept of how we commonly associate freedom with social success and financial security. Yet it is a statement that cannot be uprooted, because success and security, in the socially accepted sense, are arbitrary terms, implying that you do not belong in this world and that somehow to belong you need to be accepted by standing on the shoulders of others who you falsely believe threaten your security.

The accepted notion of success is to assume that our very existence is wrong and that somehow we need to make it right. If your psychological center of gravity were corrected so you understood that "you" existing in this world is itself a miracle, and thus already successful beyond words, then the magic and beauty of our world would unfold purely because the success we were seeking we already intrinsically owned. This clarified reality of success comes only to those who are already completely free in this life. But this raises the question, what does it mean to be completely free in this life?

The mystery that we encounter in our endeavor toward freedom in this life has nothing fundamentally to do with success and security, as these are intrinsic attributes arising out of the knowledge that one already possesses what one once searched for. But instead, that which is within our original nature is enlightenment, the completely free state, to which this book is dedicated. The idea that we already possess enlightenment is still not generally accepted among those who strive to achieve this state of consciousness. In the same fashion that an athlete sets out goals and trains hard to achieve them, so too do many who are spiritually charged toward liberation in this life. Paradoxically, though, we cannot be enlightened without the undying thirst and hunger for enlightenment. This is called the highest desire within our wisdom traditions.

If one understands this state of enlightenment and what is being said here in a lazy sense, then it will be like waiting in Sydney for a train from New York to Los Angeles: it will simply not arrive, and one will be lost in time, rather than enlightenment striking like lightning. This common understanding of enlightenment becomes time-bound in a linear thought structure in exactly the same way that success and security are thought to be acquired in the future.

This perception of enlightenment within the field of time poses many difficult ideas of what it means to be liberated, and these ideas themselves are obstacles to true liberation. The main difficulty to overcome is that those who strive for enlightenment unknowingly assign it the quality of a temporary state rather than everlasting. Striving for enlightenment does ascribe to it the temporal order of the universe, because anything in the field of time is an illusionary concept of past or future, which ultimately distracts our attention from the reality of the present moment. This is known as *samsara* (संसार) in Sanskrit, referring to the wheel of time, which is thought to be an illusion. In revealing our time-bound concept of enlightenment, it is extremely hard for most of us to swallow, for the sheer fact that enlightenment is the eternal aspect deep within our consciousness that is a reflection of the eternal universe. We tend to try and grasp such axiomatic truths with our intellect, which is itself a time-bound instrument of discernment, and in most cases the result of time. This is not to insult the intellect, but rather it is the recognition that if our intuitive faculties have not opened up, then the intellect has little to no chance of peering into the esoteric heart of the universe that lies beyond the temporal scope. American occultist William Walker Atkinson, writing under the pseudonym Yogi Ramacharaka in the classic *Lessons in Gnani Yoga* states:

And, the Intellect experiences a similar difficulty when it tries to think of an Eternal—a That which is above and outside of Time. We see Time in operation everywhere, and take it for granted that Time is a reality—an actual thing. But this is a mistake of the senses. There is no such thing as Time, in reality. Time exists solely in our minds. It is merely a form of perception by which we express our consciousness of the Change of Things.

We cannot think of Time except in connection with a succession of changes of things in our consciousness—either things of the outer world, or the passing of thought-things through our mind. A day is merely the consciousness of the passing of the sun—an hour or minute merely the subdivision of the day, or else the consciousness of the movement of the hands of the clock—merely the consciousness of the movement of Things—the symbols of changes in Things. In a world without changes in Things, there would be no such things as Time. Time is but a mental invention. Such is the report of the Intellect.[1]

In Sanskrit the essence of eternity within the individual's consciousness is known as Atman (आत्मन्) and the universal essence of eternity underlying and within the nature of things is known as Brahman (ब्रह्मन्), the Ultimate Reality. Yoga is the union of both Atman and Brahman, as yoga originates from the Sanskrit root *yuj,* which means to yoke, unite, or join with the absolute Ultimate Reality/irreducible essence of the universe, similar to the concepts of God in the West, the irreducible essence of the Tao in China, Allah in the Muslim world, and so on. Patañjali, the great sage of Indian antiquity, articulates this more simply in his epic *Yoga-Sūtra*. The first sutra (1.1) states:

Now, the teachings of yoga.[2]

The point Patañjali is attempting to express in this sutra is that *right now,* completely in this present moment, is where our consciousness is enlightened in union with the irreducible essence of the universe. Not five minutes from now, tomorrow, or at a future date, but instead, right here and now. This should be fundamental, common sense in our world, yet all systems of knowledge are put into a framework of time. But if enlightenment is the eternal essence of our consciousness, how could eternity be anywhere else but now? Enlightenment could not be associated with any framework of time, as we will continue to discover throughout this book. How then could we strive for something that is right here in our possession? There is no way that we could. But the world we are all brought into overemphasizes its focus upon social success and material wealth, which keeps our attention fixed on the future. This perspective limits our mind because we are molded to believe we are each separate, a view that increases our anxious belief of not belonging to life. Anything associated with time only perpetuates this belief and is a key contributor to the underlying anxiety of our civilization. Any framework of time, then, must be limited as it is in correspondence with the temporal aspect of the universe, samsara. On the other hand, enlightenment is limitless and corresponds to the eternal aspect of the universe that is eclipsed by samsara. This eternal resonance in our consciousness is known in Sanskrit as *nirvana* (निर्वाण), the enlightened mind. Yet, even the Sanskrit nirvana is thought of in terms of time and a striving for enlightenment.

Nirvana is a word used extensively in Buddhism with the upmost of reverence. But even in Buddhism, nirvana is thought of in the framework of time. Especially in Theravada and Mahayana Buddhism, one is taught to chase after enlightenment as if it is some future event. In following this method, a monk replicates a dog chasing its own tail, and in doing so, never actually arrives because the point of arrival is "here and now."

Zen, the most recognized Buddhism in Japan, also treats enlightenment in the sense of time through the practice of *zazen*. Zazen is a way of trying to induce a permanent state of enlightenment upon the mind of the monk, which again implies that we do not already possess enlightenment. Though this is the modern perspective of Zen in Japan, it was not the original Zen that washed onto their shores from China, Tibet, and Nepal, and before that, from India originally. The original Zen was wholly concerned with the realization that enlightenment is an innate aspect of our consciousness, which is why many of the original masters of Zen, such as Bodhidharma, always emphasized the importance to their students of giving up the search for enlightenment because it cannot be acquired in the same way we acquire beliefs or purchase a new garment. Not only the masters of Zen, but almost all masters of Eastern and Western contemplative spiritual traditions as well, believe that enlightenment exists outside of time and in eternity, which exists in the ever-present now.

The original practice of Zen means to be completely absorbed in the eternal now, which brings the contemplative wisdom of enlightenment to the forefront of one's pure mind. The word *Zen* in Japanese actually refers to that contemplative enlightened state, which derives from the Japanese pronunciation of the Middle Chinese word *chan* (禪) and in turn is derived from *dhyana* (ध्यान) in Sanskrit which can be translated as "absorption," "concentration," or "meditative state." Zen, then, means to be completely absorbed in the present moment in everything we experience in life. Zen in conversation, Zen in art, Zen in eating, Zen in making love, Zen in meditation, and Zen in going to the toilet. No matter what our experience is, it is Zen if there really is only the eternal now.

The biggest problem that exists not only in Buddhism, but also in life in general, is that we seek to induce a state of consciousness that already is our original nature. Our mind, caught in the details of time, cannot perceive this original nature because it is obscured by social, cultural, religious, and egotistical conditioning. When we seek what we already have, we prevent ourselves from perceiving the eternal in all things through the original state of enlightenment. We feel distant and cut off from eternity, so we seek any method to induce enlightenment. We practice meditation, yoga, t'ai chi, qigong, lucid dreaming, mindfulness; we take psychedelics; or we sit at the feet of a guru. All of this is a form of spiritual postponement, meaning that we are continually putting off our enlightenment to feel as though we are doing something good and noble from striving.

Tantric Buddhism shares some of the same basic philosophical underpinnings of Zen. The tenth-century tantric work of Saraha expresses this point:

> If it [the Truth] is already manifest, what's the use of
>   meditation?
> And if it is hidden, one is just measuring darkness.
> Mantras and tantras, meditation and concentration,
> They are all a cause of self-deception.
> Do not defile in contemplation thought that is pure in
>   its own nature,
> But abide in the bliss of yourself and cease those
>   torments.
> Whatever you see, that is it,
> In front, behind, in all the ten directions.
> Even today let your master make an end of delusion!
> The nature of the sky is originally clear,
> But by gazing and gazing the sight becomes obscured.[3]

Zen, like Taoism, explains that there is a unique naturalness to enlightenment because the individual has stepped out of the illusion of a past and future, and instead fallen into the eternal way of the now—or to use Taoist terminology, way of the Tao. When we do not try to induce enlightenment, we fall into accord with nature. The reason for this is because nature's patterns, principles, and essential reality are in the pure stillness of the eternal now. Nature cannot be yesterday or tomorrow; it can only be now. Humanity must realize that we are also nature, and what constitutes nature's reality constitutes ours. There is not nature on the one hand and humanity on the other. We are nature, and because we have the assumption that we are not, we destroy nature as if we were its lords. Isolating ourselves from nature breeds unnecessary anxiety, because we are perpetually obsessed with survival rather than the reality of belonging to nature and thriving as a result. Our impetus toward survival is rooted in our expectations of the future based on our experiences of the past. The stress of survival has nothing to do with the Zen mind absorbed in the present moment.

The understanding that we belong to nature and that we can trust the universe arises in the consciousness of one who is absorbed in the eternal now of enlightenment. This absorption is a complete and thorough comprehension that enlightenment is innately ours right now and nowhere else. Despite saying all this, the vast majority of us, in fact, do not truly feel it. Others may feel it, but it is a temporary state that comes and goes according to our experiences. Nevertheless, we do slip in and out of being completely conscious in the reality of the present moment, which is explored within this book.

I am mindful, though, that something as deep and profound as the enlightenment that is experienced in the present moment can be superficially understood by the discursive intellect. In all sincere self-work practiced by those interested in the great work of eternity, a subtle state of consciousness and perception known as the *intellectual intuition* develops within the sincere seeker of truth. This allows one to delve into the esoteric heart of the mystery veiled in temporal form. *Enlightenment Now* is not like any of the multitude of New Age materials that pacify the individual with a superficial understanding of enlightenment and the eternal now, one that the wine connoisseur would say "lacks body." On the contrary, this book will give an extensive study of the philosophical, psychological, metaphysical, and spiritual implications of what remaining completely present in the state of enlightenment actually means and how it is really the only state of being. This will also reveal how it is a social and cultural imperative to live in the now.

My wish in this book is to reveal the esoteric heart of enlightenment so we can all bask in the eternal sunshine from within. This book itself exists within time, yet the inspiration and artistry of this book is of an order beyond the realm of time. I am not saying here that I myself dwell in eternity and so therefore I could write this book. Rather, I mean that any form of art is inspired and comes from that eternal spontaneity beyond time and space, which is an intelligence that you and I are an aspect of. Yet, the irony is that any piece of art—no matter whether it is writing, music, painting, gardening, or any other art—can only be experienced, felt, and understood within the field of time. Art is the result of time and eternity fusing together. It is as if an artist has found a way to bring postcards back from eternity and present them using our limited instruments of time, no matter whether that is a pen or paintbrush. As an artist brings the eternal into temporal reality, a sage in the same resonant quality of an artist can perceive the eternal in the realm of time. The prolific writer and mystical philosopher Aldous Huxley gives credence to this enlightened state within *The Perennial Philosophy:*

For the fully enlightened, totally liberated person, *samsara* and *nirvana,* time and eternity, the phenomenal and the Real, are essentially one. His whole life is an unsleeping and one-pointed contemplation of the Godhead in and through the things, lives, minds and events of the world becoming. There is here no mutation of the soul, no atrophy of any of its powers and capacities. Rather, there is a general enhancement and intensification of consciousness, and at the same time an extension and transfiguration.[4]

This understanding of time and eternity, samsara and nirvana, together and essentially one, is usually isolated to the consciousness of a sage or an artist who is enlightened in the spontaneity of the eternal now. But this mutual relationship between time and eternity will be of key importance throughout this book, and it also will be thoroughly dissected.

For the human experience of enlightenment and an absorption in the eternal now, one needs the realm of time but is not dependent on the distractive aspects of time and the limitations they tend to evoke in our mind. To a master, the temporal order of the universe is the crest of a wave that belongs to an eternal ocean. So *Enlightenment Now* is not a critique of time, as without time we could not experience eternity or even read this book. Yet, the reality of eternity has been co-opted by religion with the notion that the eternal realm, known by the religious as heaven, is a place that we go to after death. This implies that religions such as Christianity, Islam, and Judaism, just to name a few, view eternity to be within the process of linear time. The relationship between time and eternity is thought of much differently in the East, especially in the Hindu and Taoist traditions. Neither of these Eastern traditions maps time in the linear sense, but instead they devised a system to understand time's nonlinear qualities in relation to matter, mind, and spirit. In Hinduism the nonlinearity of time is broken down into the *yuga* cycles, which map the consciousness that drives the process of linear time. The yugas, then, are an epoch or era within a four age cycle that each contain different characteristics, beginning with Satya Yuga (ideal or truthful/spiritual age), Treta Yuga (virtue declined by a quarter/mental age), Dvapara Yuga (virtue declined by half/energy age), and finally Kali Yuga (virtue reduced to a quarter/material age). Also in Taoism we have the I Ching, or Book of Changes in English, the epic text from the Chinese sages of antiquity. This book of Taoist wisdom attempts to know the nonlinear patterns of time that we experience in our inner and outer worlds through their relationship to the eternal irreducible essence of the universe known as Tao in Chinese.

Both Hinduism and Taoism present the question, How could eternity be a linear construct if it is ever-present, everlasting, and all enduring, without beginning or end? Where could eternity be—or enlightenment experienced—other than right now? Those who are sincere in liberation are usually the only ones who know the answers to such questions through their own experience. One who is sincere in realizing liberation usually slips into a world beyond the normal conventional way of thinking. This world beyond convention is the Middle Way of the Buddha, Lao-tzu's Way of the Tao, the Great Work of Gnosticism, the Royal Road, and the Hermetic Art of Alchemy. The world beyond convention, which is the integration of the physical, mental, and spiritual planes of consciousness into one, dawns upon the consciousness of one sincere in the great work of eternity.

In Scholastic philosophy, the Medieval Latin neologism *aeviternitas* or *aeviternal* describes a state of consciousness that an individual experiences where time and eternity are one. The sages of ancient and contemporary times dwell in this aeviternal state of consciousness, meaning they exist on the cusp where eternity (nirvana) and time (samsara) meet—or we should more accurately say are one. This aeviternal state is the proper position for a human being's consciousness, as we are the bridge between heaven (formless reality) and earth (the world of form). "Right now" is where they meet and are one. But standing in the way of this recognition are all the linear limitations of time that have hypnotized us into believing they are real, which only veils our connection to eternity.

Enlightenment Now is a way of dehypnotizing our linear constraints so we can finally reconnect to the real world, which we actually know little about. In revealing this real world, that aeviternal state will be realized within the individual, and in doing so, eternity will come back into the field of time through *now*.

1
Monarchical View of the Universe

TO SET OUT ON A JOURNEY to arrive at a destination where we already are is surely an absurd act. In the eyes of an individual liberated in this life (called a *jivanmukta* in Sanskrit), it is almost comical to watch humanity go around and around on the wheel of ignorance and suffering, because humanity's ignorance and suffering is a result of a search for something we already have. To those jivanmuktas who have graced the earth, enlightenment is our innate way of being, and freedom is our inherent way of life, in response to enlightenment. Freedom and enlightenment go hand in hand, as they mutually arise in the same way that the universe produces consciousness and consciousness evokes the universe. If freedom and enlightenment are our natural birthright, why do most of us not feel this state of liberation? The way of being and life we have invested all of our energy into is incompatible with an individual's enlightenment and the freedom of the collective.

In the general sense, enlightenment and freedom are inconceivable, and somehow both exist as a state of consciousness isolated to those dwelling in forests and places of sacred worship. We tend to have such generalizations of life because we feel isolated and cut off from the world. We believe we aren't worthy of experiencing life in its fullest expression. "Little me, poor little me. Why should I be of any special value?" This type of self-pity is the accepted mantra of the human race, and to step beyond your own worth issues is frowned upon by others, who lack the coherence and foresight to see their own self-loathing. Surely we must admit that this attitude toward life, other people, and ourselves is a form of psychosis so ingrained that we lack the awareness to uproot its hypnosis. In not feeling worthy, we pass this on to our children, and then they do the same to their children. It goes on generation after generation without cessation. In truth, we are psychologically abusing our children and all other people with our own projection of worthlessness. Our orientation of reality is obscured by our habit of projecting our own internal issues on others rather than looking within to work through the hypnosis that blurs our vision of reality.

This disorientation is the result of the individual feeling subservient to the world and other people. Feeling subservient causes a ripple effect of people projecting their frustrated and suppressed nature upon others whom they assume are in a lesser position in life. Woven into the fabric of society and culture is this yearning to be in a "kingly" position above the rest. We seek this position because our assumption of life and everything that is part of it is based on the idea that intrinsic to the nature of reality are monarchical systems that are built around a ruler, leader, or lord. This way of thinking is a political analogy of the universe where even God is a dictator. As a result the concept of monarchy becomes an entrenched way of thinking that is applied to families, friendships, governments, society, religions, business, the universe, and even reality itself. A result of this perception is the current world we live in now. But is this how reality truly *is*?

THE WAY OF MONARCHICAL CONSCIOUSNESS

If we continue to assume that reality is of a monarchical nature, how could individual peace of mind and collective equality ever come about? Both are impossible from the monarchical standpoint, yet we consistently perpetuate this mode of consciousness as if it were superior because many people perceive reality only superficially. So, a rank within a hierarchy is thought to be a position of power that deserves respect. The tendency in many civilizations has been that most individuals cannot control such admiration toward themselves, so they abuse their power, and in doing so, ultimately fall from power only to be replaced by another individual who rises to attempt the same process. It is a never-ending cycle caused by how we perceive reality as a monarchical order. This perception of life as a monarchical order has become so indoctrinated into humanity that we do not even question its authenticity. In fact, many people have lost the ability to question most things in life because they feel they do not belong to life. Thinking that one is lower on the scale of life has a ripple effect in the way we perceive reality in a hierarchical framework. In revealing this, the very way we perceive reality and ourselves is corrupted and fails to serve us. If perceiving reality in this way does not serve us, then why do we perpetually uphold it?

Our history is plagued with this monarchical view of life. We are so conditioned with this view that we passively acquiesce to anybody who has an apparent hierarchical position. Whether in the workplace, religion, nation, family, or anywhere else, many people unconsciously submit their whole being to whom or what they believe to be on a higher level. Now let's not confuse this passivity with authentic humility and receptivity. This passivity that many people exhibit results from conformity—in the same way that sheep follow the herd—rather than seeking to find the source of one's submissive attitude through questioning our conditioning. Authentic humility and receptivity are beyond our conditioned limitations, as they are the latent human virtues that can never be contrived. But we are prevented from manifesting these virtues by a quagmire of conditioning, which causes one to perceive oneself in a lowly position within a hierarchy, instead of in relation to the universe. The virtues of humility and receptivity do not come to fruition through the monarchical view of reality. So again, why do we uphold a state of consciousness that does not serve us? How far back in history did we begin perceiving reality in the sense of hierarchy? When did we develop the concept that we can be in a lower position of life than another?

HISTORY OF THE MONARCHICAL VIEW

Tracing our history back to pre-agrarian culture, humanity was a people living in and with nature. We existed in small tribal and shamanic communities taking only the necessities of life, rather than whatever we wanted. Those archaic cultures did not have to seek equilibrium with the environment because they were already naturally harmonious. They perceived nature in all of its glory, as an extension of themselves, instead of our modern approach to nature as a separate and tyrannical lord. Material acquisitions were of no importance, as the welfare of the individual *and* the community were the main priorities.

This is not to say that these cultures were above individual and collective folly, but the stark difference to our modern civilization is that their faults were generally addressed with an attempt to heal any problem through a consensus of opinion in a communal setting. An individual's problem was the community's problem and vice versa. The welfare of one was the welfare of all. In such a model, there is no individual above the others who decides what is good for the people. Even the rise of the shaman and holy person did not threaten this communal importance within tribal cultures. The shaman and holy person, though, is respected as the one who has done the internal work to possess the innate wisdom that heals others' physical and psychological ailments. This is not to say that a shaman or a holy person necessarily held a position of authority over the community. On the contrary, in most cases the shaman and holy person was a hunter and gatherer just like anyone else, but differed in having a keen interest in medicine and healing, in much the same way that certain women of the community had a keen interest in arts and crafts.

In this statement we are not suggesting that only men were shamans or holy people and that only women were interested in arts and crafts; that would be a common mistaken assumption. Within many tribal communities in ancient times the shaman and holy person, either female or male, held a place of equal importance to other members of the tribe, which is hard for us to fathom in our current era from a state of consciousness that tends to perceive reality in the mold of layers and levels of hierarchy.

There were tribes in ancient times that did kill and shun shamans or holy people as outsiders. But in many cases tribal communities were based on the natural philosophy of mutuality as opposed to the modern view of individuality because individuality had not blossomed as it has in our current era. Tribal cultures are traditionally a partnership society based on mutuality and anyone in those ancient times who sought individual salvation from the group ran the risk of nature's wrath. Those who were not mutually in sync with the other people of the tribe were viewed to disturb its harmony. Individuality, then, in those times was about how one benefited the group. Everybody had their place within the community by following what their natural God-given talents were. No one had to be assigned duties, as there was no one in the role of a dictator in the community assigning duties to others.

In the Taoist philosophy of China, each and every individual has his or her own unique psychosomatic pattern that they express either physically or psychologically, which ultimately brings harmony to the world. In Chinese this unique organic pattern is known as *li* (理), and by following your li you naturally harmonize with the universal essence and order, Tao (道), which brings harmonic resonance into the world of form, known as *ying* (應) in Chinese. The ancient Taoist sages understood the natural tribal values brought down from living with nature and then into agrarian society. Invariably our li, in other words, our intrinsic human nature, is linked to art, because art in its purest form is the self-expression of one's organic pattern. Because of this, the artistic path calls to the artist, and is not the result of personal desires and perceived pleasures.

Pursuing your personal desires and pleasures within the apparently secure confines of your own physical and psychological comfort zones is no way to discover your organic pattern or freedom. This vain pursuit actually has more in common with a prison than anything else. That calling which naturally dawns upon our mind is the path of the hero, if we choose not to be distracted by what our egotistical mind is attracted to, because the ego is invariably associated to the hypnosis of laziness and procrastination. Mythologist and philosopher Joseph Campbell beautifully called following this calling "the Hero's Journey." He adeptly explained that if you discover your li and follow it—"following your bliss" in Campbell's terminology—then you not only continually grow along the path of life, but you also change the world through your self-expression as it harmonizes with everything in reality, that is, ying. For example, artists often have the ying ability to bring people together, move them emotionally, and inspire others. Ironically, though, a lot of people strive to become an artist for fame or to appease their own intellectual pursuits and in both cases they usually fall short of the mark. On the other hand, successful artists in a lot of cases never intended to be famous and weren't originally passionate about their craft, but from following the intuitive calling of li along the hero's journey they continue to grow and become extremely passionate without any intention to do so at the outset.

Establishing harmony between the individual and the community was common etiquette among many ancient natural tribal cultures. The community was an extension of the individual and so the individual is the community. The inner life of the individual becomes the culture. The microcosm and macrocosm are both one and the same. This view is shared in Traditional Chinese Medicine (TCM) where the small picture and the big picture are the same picture, which means the world is a reflection of what is happening in the inner life of the individual. The knowledge attained from this way of life is that if you want to change the community you have to change yourself, as the community is the result of many individuals. This is still the way life is now, and it can never deviate from this course because any community, no matter how large or small, is always the outcome of the individual. But something in those ancient times compelled those small tribes to grow and merge into larger communities with ultimately larger problems. We deviated from the natural course of following our natural talents, and as a result were thrust into assigned duties. As larger communities continued to grow, the necessities for living became increasingly scarce as a result. Commonplace aspects of tribal life had to be changed or cast aside.

The greatest change of those times was when our way of life went from living harmoniously with nature to the formation of agrarian cultures. This was the beginning of individuals giving their innate power over to a society that molded them into conforming with what it needs to function. Agrarian culture is more mechanical than humanistic, so for such a society to operate sufficiently its components—the people—need to be assigned specific duties to maintain the cultural framework.

Pursuing one's natural creative calling, which eventually brought harmony to the community, became a distant memory as the people suppressed such desires in favor of money attained for their labor, which supplied them the means to purchase food, clothing, and shelter. These means, which were once our natural right, became a commodity run by the society. Because of that, we as individuals lost our sense of responsibility, because the society and culture took over our responsibility in the role of a parental figure. A lack of responsibility leads to passive conformity—and not the receptiveness of humility, but instead a docile passivity more like that of a zombie than anything else. Instead of a society and culture acting in accord with the individual mind, the individual begins to take on the functions of the society and culture, resulting in the average human being living their everyday life as mere machines. We take on the machinelike operations of the society and culture in all aspects of our life. In the modern era, many people are not conscious of this machinelike behavior because it has become so ingrained into the psyche that they never question its authenticity.

Since the beginning of agrarian cultures these machinelike habits and tendencies of the individual took over our natural self-expression. Instead of communal values based on individual artistic satisfaction, we took on an assigned and a somewhat slavery orientated division of labor and a division of function within the society to keep the social engine running like a well-oiled machine.

In our mechanical model of a linear world, the external order begins to dictate a way of life to the individual, which is in reality artificial. A conformist society begins when we relinquish our power away to a machine that is unnatural and devoid of life. This passive conformity can be traced back to the origins of the Hindu caste system and medieval Western Christian society under the feudal system.

When a settled agrarian culture is born, such as the ancient Hindu and Christian societies, they tend to build a township not only to protect people from outside influences, but also to develop a mental framework based on rules and regulations that one should abide by. A division of labor and division of function is the result of the complexity of an agrarian culture. From this division, the ancient Hindus of the Vedic civilization developed a caste system to assign the labor and function of society. The Hindu caste is made up of the Brahmins (priesthood), Kshatriyas (nobility), Vaishyas (merchants and farmers), and the Shudras (laborers). A direct reflection of this caste system is that of the medieval Christian society under the feudal system, where we have the priesthood of the church, feudal lords and royalty of nobility, farmers and merchants of the commons, and the serfs who were the slaves. This pattern is still with us today, as when we are born into this world we come out of nature and are taught to submit to a caste and rule of society and culture.

This is the crucifixion of the individual and the sacrifice we all suffer. According to the tyranny of the machine, this crucifixion is for the "common good." But there is a stark difference between the Hindu and Christian societies of ancient times, and that difference is that once a Hindu has fulfilled their duties for society in this life, they are allowed to break away from caste and become a sage in the forest, which is loathed by Christian society as one is thought of as useless if they do not contribute to the social order. This break away from caste is viewed as a return back to nature and could be thought of as a resurrection. A sage is not moved by the social mind and its motives and so they do not conform to its rule. Jesus was a sage in this mold, and is why he was not thought of as a particularly good member of society and he was actually put to death by such a deluded conformist society. Those who submit lose their natural innocence.

Our submission to rule annihilates the freedom that is innately ours. In such a structure of submission, enlightenment is something one can only ponder in the hope of experiencing it in later life according to the Hindu caste system. But as we see in modern-day India, the life of a *vanaprastha* (Sanskrit for an individual living in the forest as a hermit after giving up material desires) is seldom taken on because its appeal has been diminished by our society and culture, which suppress individual spiritual liberation. From the inception of agrarian culture until now, the society and culture dictate life toward the individual. We develop a subtle psychosis from trying to tiptoe our whole life within the prisonlike confines of the rules and regulations that keep the machine ticking.

This form of social and cultural suppression, as we see with the ancient Hindu caste system, evolved from groups of people attaining positions of power, such as the Brahmins (priesthood) and Kshatriyas (nobility). It would be hard for us to speculate how this all occurred. But our world now is the outgrowth of that original conception. From the beginnings of this hierarchy the average individual is made to feel subordinate to the higher classes. And so we develop this view that life is governed from above. This view is in stark contrast to how life was within pre-agrarian tribal communities, because they were part of a group consensus who all belonged to nature. The governing-from-above view of life infiltrated all aspects of society, culture, and religion. All the way from the highest ranks to the lowest, people have this idea of a governing system of control from above.

Religions were quick to adopt this system of authority. Our spirituality coming out of the natural world was molded into a tool of indoctrinated belief to rule the population. According to Sigmund Freud, the Egyptian pharaoh Akhenaten, known as Amenhotep IV before the fifth year of his reign, who Freud suggests is the pioneer of a monotheistic religion that Moses was probably a follower of, spawned the concept that the universe is governed from above. As a result of this common belief, the universe took on the role as a governor and lawgiver from above. The ancient Persians had a tradition of "king of kings," which came from Darius I (550–486 BCE). This tradition is based on a kingly God lording over the world, which is the essence of a political analogy of the universe that many kings throughout history employed to maintain control of the masses. During that time, the idea of a king of kings was a foreign way of looking at the universe, and was diametrically opposed to the thought of China, Greece, India, and the great philosophers of those civilizations of that time, most notably Lao-tzu, Pythagoras, Gautama the Buddha, and Confucius. It does not matter whether we were living in Egypt, Babylon, Chaldea, India, or anywhere else, because the king of kings tradition became a social norm that one should adhere to. As a result of this belief, we began to think of God as a king, along with the idea that "he" punishes us for our sins. The irony here is that what we perceive as sins are only judged as such according to what is not accepted for the beneficial upkeep of the society, culture, and religion.

If God is all-loving, why would she/he/it punish its children or cause them any harm intentionally? We are again giving away our sense of responsibility here, because we expect God to punish us *for* our sins, rather than admitting that we are punished *by* our sins. This differs vastly from Eastern wisdom. In the East we discover the law of *karma,* which is based on the obvious phenomena of actions and their processes of cause and effect. The major difference is that according to the principle of karma there is no good or bad, as these are personal judgments that differ among individuals. But instead karma aligns with the age-old phrase "you reap what you sow." This also corresponds to the sixth principle in Hermeticism:

VI. THE PRINCIPLE OF CAUSE AND EFFECT

Every Cause has its Effect; every Effect has its Cause; everything happens according to Law; Chance is but a name for Law not recognized; there are many planes of causation, but nothing escapes the Law.[1]

Law in Hermetic terminology is not to be thought of as a governing apparatus in the sense of a law giver from above. But rather it is a natural flux of the universe and consciousness that keeps reality harmonious, which is actually in alignment with the Chinese Tao and Sanskrit Brahman. Inquiring into this, we discover that the monarchical view of reality has developed far more in Western religions than those of the East. For example, in the West we think of God as a "creator" of the universe in the kingly sense, as how one would govern from above. Yet in the East there is still a relationship to nature, because in most spiritual paths of the East they view the universe as an organism that grows without any aspect of monarchy, as monarchy is a human concept. A child in Europe, for instance, may ask her mother, "How was I made?" but in China a child may ask her mother, "How did I grow?"

The fundamental differences between the Eastern and Western views of the universe can be attributed to the Book of Genesis. According to Genesis the universe is "made" in the same way that a carpenter builds a house. The world is an artifact from the hands of an all-governing creator God. Remember how we are all taught that Jesus was the son of a carpenter, which is actually an allegory, because Jesus was also the son of God (creator or carpenter). This model of the universe is what British philosopher Alan Watts called "the ceramic model of the universe."

Christianity and its thousands of sects are based heavily on the principle of God as creator of the universe. This is why most Christians think of God or Jesus as a king. In *The Book of Common Prayer* it states:

> *O Lord our heavenly Father, high and mighty, King*
> *of kings, Lord of lords, the only Ruler of princes, who*
> *dost from thy throne behold all the dwellers upon*
> *earth.*[2]

The effect of kingly worship leads people to relate to the world as if they were subjects under a king. The church is based on this monarchical theory with the Pope on his throne and also in how the leader of the congregation can come across as a tyrant wielding the fear of God rather than as a holy man. A great Catholic cathedral, for instance, is known as a *basilica*, a Latin word that derives from the Greek *basileios stoa*, meaning both a "Royal *Stoa*" (ancient Greek architecture) and a tribunal chamber for a king. So a basilica is a house fit for a king, such as the Pope, for example. On top of this, the ritual of the Catholic Church is based on the court rituals of Byzantium.

In direct relation to this kingly place of worship, the Protestant Church is built on the same principle as a judicial courthouse. Both Catholic and Protestant architectural structures are built on a monarchical and political view of the universe. All of this disassociates the individual from the church and ultimately from God. The monarchical view of the universe suggests that there is a difference between the maker and made, creator and created, and so on. As we have stated, this model originated from cultures whose governments were monarchical.

This assumption of a difference between maker and made is upheld by the established authority of our time, whether that be religion, nation, government, corporate, banking or commerce. To define and promote the apparent difference between creator and created benefits such institutions because people erroneously believe the status quo, which tells them they are only an effect rather than a cause. This perception results from the concept that we are made in the same way that a carpenter builds a house with his hands, meaning anything that is created results from work performed from the outside inward, as a sculptor carves wood. Again, this is vastly different from the perception of the original tribal cultures, and also the wisdom of the East, because there the universe is perceived as an organism that grows. So when we watch anything that grows in nature it manifests from the inside out, as a flower blossoms and expands from a simple humble bud.

We do not necessarily need to debate about this natural growth fact, because this is the way things are in nature. All organisms are in accord with this natural growth pattern from the inside out. Yet the human mind has been conditioned into the opposite perspective of the monarchical view of reality since the dawn of agrarian culture. As a result, control and force have been substituted for organic growth. Even within our human body we feel the effects of this monarchical view.

PSYCHOPHYSICAL MONARCHY

A state of monarchy within the human body and mind begins subtly at a young age. Many people go through their entire life without becoming conscious of it. Since this view is the norm within the world, we have lost the ability to listen to our body and its needs. Many people usually only listen to what their mind wants, with no consideration for the bodily needs. We have lost the ability to listen and feel with our stomachs, and instead we only listen, feel, and eat with what stimulates our mind's desires. Our culture promotes only the chattering ego in our mind because when one is locked into the repetitive cycle of the ego seeking pleasures, which is good for a society's economic bottom line. Obesity and all sorts of biological and psychological diseases result from listening only to what the spoiled kid inside of us—the ego—wants.

From childhood we are not taught anything about that constant chatter within our head, because our parents and schools are none the wiser. They are still victims of this internal monarchy. The king in the psychophysical sense is the ego, and the innocent victim under its rule is the physical body. In relation to social, cultural, and religious monarchy, it is interesting that, because of the rule and suppression of the individual, we develop a subtle psychosis in the mind in the same fashion that a body develops illness from eating unhealthy food.

Our ego governs the body without listening to the body's internal needs. The ego functions on the monarchical view from the outside inward, so it only seeks what it perceives as pleasure without consulting the body. The ego governs the body like a king governs the world. But if this view of reality is fraught with sickness on all levels, how could it be natural? How could we uphold such a view without question? As we mentioned, an organism grows "of itself" from inside outward in perfect harmony, like a flower in full bloom. The psychophysical body of our organism is no different from a flower or any other organism. Relating this to the body, neither the brain nor the stomach is the boss, because they mutually depend upon each other. Everything in our body is interdependent, as our brain sends an electrical signal to the hand to put food in our mouth to go into the stomach to nourish the organs which gives the hand its function and the brain its ability to think.

The government of our body is not monarchical, but instead, it is self-governing, organic, without the need for assigning specific duties to our organs. Without assigning duty, our body is perfectly harmonious, especially if the mind and body are realized to be one and the same. The body and the mind being one is a core principle within Taoism and Zen Buddhism, which many spiritual paths overlook in their primary focus on only the mind. Our psychophysical organism is a testament to the way things were in pre-agrarian cultures. There is no need for any form of dictatorship, as we belong to this world.

The monarchical view of the universe has put humanity in a spin disconnecting us from our natural place within the cosmos. In pre-agrarian cultures, certainly not everything was rosy, but the difference between now and then is that most people acknowledged their own innate power and uniqueness. The desire of many pre-agrarian cultures was to have collective equality and individual equanimity.

Enlightenment was not thought of as a distant, high abode where only those who have reached this state are accepted by God. The ones who were not distracted by the drama of life in those times understood that what we seek we already are.

The rise of the Hindu Vedas and Upanishads is the evidence of this fact, as those scriptures continually hum into the mind like a lullaby *tat tvam asi,* a Sanskrit phrase meaning "thou art That." The origins of the pre-Hindu caste system arose from those texts, which were spoken verbally before becoming written texts and may be older even than the ancient Indus Valley civilization. *Tat tvam asi,* you are That now, Atman which is Brahman, according to those forest dwellers of antiquity. In the ancient sacred song of the *Chandogya Upanishad* we discover the story of Svetaketu, who is the son of the great sage Uddalaka. Svetaketu asks Uddalaka (who is "Sir" in this discourse) about the nature of his existence and that what we seek we already *are,* which corresponds to the Eastern view of growth:

> *"Bring me a fruit of that banyan tree."*
> *"Here it is, venerable Sir."*
> *"Break it."*
> *"It is broken, venerable Sir."*
> *"What do you see there?"*
> *"These seeds, exceedingly small."*
> *"Break one of these, my son."*
> *"It is broken, venerable Sir."*
> *"What do you see there?"*
> *"Nothing at all, venerable Sir."*
> *The father said: "That subtle essence, my dear, which*
> *you do not perceive there—from that very essence*
> *this great banyan arises. Believe me, my dear.*
> *Now, that which is the subtle essence—in it all*
> *that exists has its self. That is the True. That is*
> *the Self. Thou art that, Svetaketu."*[3]

The monarchical view of the universe is diametrically opposed to teaching people that the enlightenment they seek is already within them. As a result, we have developed in our religious and spiritual paths the notion that attaining enlightenment is an initiatory process existing in layers upon layers of understanding. We are made to feel that we are not "That," so we should suffer in life as a consequence on the path toward enlightenment. The monarchical view of the universe corrupts even the eventual reality of our enlightenment.

2
A Superficial Initiation
into the Future

THOSE HUMBLE SAGES who dwelled in nature as one with the natural order continued to express *tat tvam asi* in the hope that society would overcome its vain strivings through the realization "thou art That." But since society is constrained by time, the awareness of *tat tvam asi* was perverted to suit the pursuit of intellectual achievements in the future. Ancient religions took hold of the sages' wisdom and used it to further their influence within society. This was primarily done by making people believe that they were not "That."

These religions then moved the mysterious enlightenment of a sage to a place we may experience after death if we have been good. It's like we're children anticipating gifts from Santa Claus, but only if we've been good. But who determines what is "good"? The parents define it as whatever they believe it to be. It is the same with the religious concept of heaven: we are deemed to have been good in life based on our obedience toward a particular faith. Society treats this as common sense, but astonishingly it is not, because we see in both cases the abuse of children by parents and the indoctrinated dogmatic abuse by a religion upon an individual's mind.

Since we came out of nature into agrarian society, we have been taught to obey the status quo in any form or we will be punished. Religion teaches the individual that if they do not obey the doctrine

27

forced upon them, then they will be deemed sinful and be punished by God. Punishment in this context is based on the beliefs of the doctrine, and that doctrine damages the psyche, imprisoning the individual by dogmas that suppress one's natural essence and vital energy. In extreme cases, the contradictions inherent in religious doctrine force the psyche into a psychotic state, leading to institutionalization. Being institutionalized means to be an obedient cog in the vast machinery of an unnatural world. Functioning as mere machines, many people believe that if they step out of formation then they should and will be punished for not contributing to the machine's operation. As a result of such indoctrination, the vast majority of humanity believes that life is suffering.

We actually become accustomed to our suffering. We feel it is a just punishment because we have done "wrong" according to the socially accepted belief system. But everything we are punished for, and all the sins we believe we've committed—these all contribute to the upkeep of the institutional power of society, culture, religion, commerce, banking, and all other components that make up an agrarian (or modern) community. It is a complete mechanical process that constructs the individual from the outside inward, as if reality itself is designed to eliminate critical thinking and individual self-expression.

Our chronic suffering in life is the outcome of suppressing the critical thinking and artistic calling that lie dormant within our mind. Disease of the psyche can only exist in this world when people have lost the ability to feel real joy—and I mean real joy, not the so-called joy people feel at the expense of others. (This latter kind of "joy" is in fact a way of silently punishing somebody else based on our narrow view of the world.) The world's disease results from the system of punishment and perpetual suffering that we all feel the need to uphold. But all punishments and suffering—individual or collective—are phenomena of linear time and have no relation to the "eternity" that religions preach because true eternity is right here and now. Certain enlightened sages of ancient times realized the source of suffering and yearned for a way out of the cycle of punishment created by society, so they could merge with eternity through the absolute axiom of *tat tvam asi*.

In a long history of agrarian society and culture, there naturally have been many who seek to escape the physical, mental, and spiritual confines of punishment and suffering in the hope of discovering the natural harmony sages experiences within their consciousness. These sages are invariably thought of as a nuisance to society because they upset the "accepted" behavior of our cultural programming. Remember, Jesus of Nazareth was not a particularly good member of society because he revealed a spiritual reality radically different from what the masses believed, which he knew we could all live by. His attitude of "love thy neighbor" was not socially accepted or thought of as practical in a busy community of people. Jesus's attitude is still not generally accepted in our modern world as many people find expressions of love more grotesque and dangerous than expressions of fear.

History also bears the scar of numerous civilizations who never fully embraced the attitude of "love thy neighbor." For example, throughout history a multitude of witch burnings are thought to have been justified because people believe witches can harm others with black magic. But in most cases, the reality is that people were labeled witches because they lived according to a spiritual world they encountered within, a world that the vast majority did not understand. The majority of what most perceive as witches are in fact more like shamanic healers than anything else. So in our ignorance of the spiritual world, we kill these people who are in fact healers for the world. Unbelievably, these witch burnings still exist today in such countries as Papua New Guinea.

On the other hand, those who in the past encountered the eternal and yet escaped social condemnation and punishment, slowly began the development of secret societies. In ancient Egypt, Chaldea, Babylon, India, and China there was the rise of what we know as "mystery schools." The students of these mystery schools were primarily focused on exploring consciousness by escaping our time-bound constraints that ultimately lead to suffering. Intellectually they had the understanding that *tat tvam asi,* "thou art That," but they possessed neither the feeling nor the intuitive perception of that exalted state of consciousness.

This is in fact a problem encountered by many spiritual seekers and esoteric students: they seek to discover that "sense of unity" within, but their intellect is not in communion with intuition; instead the intellect is merely an instrument of time. The mystery schools existed within society, and were unable to physically escape society in the same way as Hindu renunciates do. So from within the machinery of society and culture, the mystery schools devised certain methods and practices to follow instead. According to the Taoist sage Chuang-tzu, there are significant advantages for spiritual realization by staying within a society as it helps overcome the motives that lead many people to suffering. The American master translator Burton Watson describes Chuang-tzu's approach to the world in the introduction to the *Complete Works of Chuang Tzu:*

> In Chuang Tzu's view, the man who has freed himself from conventional standards of judgment can no longer be made to suffer, for he refuses to recognize poverty as any less desirable than affluence, to recognize death as any less desirable than life. He does not in any literal sense withdraw and hide from the world—to do so would show that he still passed judgment upon the world. He remains within society but refrains from acting out of the motives that lead ordinary men to struggle for wealth, fame, success, or safety. He maintains a state that Chuang Tzu refers to as *wu-wei,* or inaction, meaning by this term not a forced quietude, but a course of action that is not founded upon any purposeful motives of gain or striving. In such a state, all human actions become as spontaneous and mindless as those of the natural world. Man becomes one with Nature, or Heaven, as Chuang Tzu calls it, and merges himself with Tao, or the Way, the underlying unity that embraces man, Nature, and all that is in the universe.[1]

And paradoxically in reading Watson's words, when we are not in the comforting environment of nature there is a propensity to experience life only through the intellect because, as we said, the intellect on its own is purely built upon the time-bound structure of society and culture. As a result, enlightenment is approached in the sense of a destination to reach, which builds the basis of an initiatory process.

INITIATION OR POSTPONEMENT

To go beyond individual and collective suffering, the mystery schools devised a systematic process of initiation that is supposed to be determined by a hierarchy of previously initiated people. This hierarchy usually determines an individual's progress based on the sincerity for truth and self-work that particular individual has. This sincerity is invariably spotted by the already initiated in the way an individual's intellect becomes receptive, and in doing so, reconnects with its unified sibling, intuition, which in esoteric terminology is known as *intellectual intuition,* a term I alluded to in the introduction.

The initiatory process was invented by the mystery schools, and maybe other older civilizations, and is still upheld by many occult and wisdom traditions of today. For an individual to follow an initiatory path is thought of as a way of acquiring knowledge on our journey into enlightenment. While the initiatory path may sometimes lead to actual enlightenment, more often than not it ends up stifling it.

For example, in Freemasonry, and especially the Scottish Rite of Freemasonry, there are thirty-three degrees of initiation that an individual must progress through. The highest degree, the thirty-third, is supposed to symbolize one who stands in the light, meaning one who is enlightened or illumined. Yet what we often discover within the degrees of Freemasonry is that those who have ascended the spiritual ladder to the thirty-third degree are in most cases not very enlightening or enlightened people at all. This is not to detract from the knowledge they have acquired, but instead it should be highlighted that in most cases, when these people have ascended to a high degree, their knowledge remains purely intellectual rather than direct *gnosis*, that is, experiential knowledge. The thirty-three degrees of Freemasonry are treated more as an educational system than anything else. Year after year one is evaluated by a hierarchy to see where one stands on the great chain of understanding. Initiation in this sense falls in line with the obedience of rites, rituals, and sacrifice, as one is not allowed to question the authority of the higher initiates.

Initiation in Freemasonry tends more toward passive obedience and dependence on the teacher and less toward individual psychological growth and spiritual enlightenment. We discover through the example of Freemasonry that on one hand there is an extraordinary intellectual development during an initiatory path, but it lacks real intuitive understanding.

Many occult and wisdom traditions, not only Freemasonry, are still subtle victims of the monarchical view of reality because the initiatory path is based on a goal to reach within the realm of time. But if you are "That" now, in the sense of *tat tvam asi,* how could enlightenment be at the end of any initiatory process? Enlightenment as an end goal comes directly from the monarchical view of the universe. For a sincere spiritual seeker and esoteric student, this is utterly confusing because we have an intellectual center that is built on the framework of time. Without access to more knowledge in regard to this matter it can be psychologically catastrophic if one begins to suppress sincere intellectual passions as a result of this time-bound oppression. The complete ignorance of psychological development leads to what American clinical psychologist John Welwood termed "spiritual bypassing." Canadian spiritual psychotherapist Robert Augustus Masters explains what this psychological problem is in his book *Spiritual Bypassing:*

> Spiritual bypassing is the use of spiritual practices and beliefs to avoid dealing with our painful feelings, unresolved wounds, and developmental needs. It is much more common than we might

think and, in fact, is so pervasive as to go largely unnoticed, except in its more obvious extremes.

Part of the reason for this is that we tend not to have very much tolerance, either personally or collectively, for facing, entering, and working through our pain, strongly preferring pain-numbing "solutions," regardless of how much suffering such "remedies" may catalyze. Because this preference has so deeply and thoroughly infiltrated our culture that it has become all but normalized, spiritual bypassing fits almost seamlessly into our collective habit of turning away from what is painful, as a kind of higher analgesic with seemingly minimal side effects. It is a spiritualized strategy not only for avoiding pain but also for legitimizing such avoidance, in ways ranging from the blatantly obvious to the extremely subtle.

Spiritual bypassing is a very persistent shadow of spirituality, manifesting in many forms, often without being acknowledged as such. Aspects of spiritual bypassing include exaggerated detachment, emotional numbing and repression, overemphasis on the positive, anger-phobia, blind or overly tolerant compassion, weak or too porous boundaries, lopsided development (cognitive intelligence often being far ahead of emotional and moral intelligence), debilitating judgment about one's negativity or shadow side, devaluation of the personal relative to the spiritual, and delusions of having arrived at a higher level of being.[2]

Spiritually inclined people have a tendency toward spiritual bypassing because they want to fix their consciousness in eternity, in the hope of avoiding personal pain, with an almost arrogant disregard toward their own individuality and the external world. Many people in this regard have only an intellectual understanding of eternity because of the sheer disregard that eternity is completely here and now within the realm of what we assume is time. This is the result of overly intellectual development arising from the monarchical view of reality. From this perspective, we are always on a journey "somewhere" and we are always busy "doing" something. The initiatory process teaches individuals to be always busy chasing a goal in the future, without saturating their consciousness in the present moment of eternal stillness. Initiation, then, is a form of "spiritual postponement," as we incorrectly believe enlightenment should be earned in the same way that an athlete achieves their goals. We continue to perpetuate our suffering by believing that we should suffer to achieve enlightenment. As we bind enlightenment to time, so will we suffer.

In the ancient mystery schools of India it was mandatory for a spiritual seeker and esoteric student to undergo twelve years of rigorous spiritual discipline. Those who attended these mystery schools in India would do numerous forms of yoga, practicing and receiving *darshan** and to check in and sit with the guru (*satsang* in Sanskrit) in a place of complete isolation from the outside world. During this process some of the students would begin spiritual development toward an authentic enlightenment quicker than others, but the master or guru would stifle that growth, supporting the monarchical perspective that they should earn it by suffering through twelve years for it. In this example, to realize enlightenment meant spending twelve years under rigorous training to arrive at a place where you already are. It does seem quite absurd, but this is what the initiatory process offers. We are always off somewhere in the future visualizing enlightenment when it is staring us right in the face here and now.

The initiatory process is an attempt to induce what is already innate in our being. The monarchical view of reality causes our mind to think in this way. To induce in one sense is to build or create, yet we can never create what is our original state of consciousness. Attempting to induce this preexisting state is not only absurd, but also will ultimately postpone one's enlightenment. Philosopher and independent scholar John Holman discusses this postponement in his book *The*

---

*Darshan is a Sanskrit word that describes a devotee's affection for a god or guru, and god's or guru's reciprocal affection for the devotee, plus continual daily blessings received from the guru.

Return of the Perennial Philosophy through the wisdom of such perennial philosophers as Ananda Coomaraswamy, Huston Smith, and
Frithjof Schuon. He states:

> Eternity means endless duration and would refer to "exoteric"
> time. Aevertinity is the "always now" (Coomaraswamy called it the
> "Nowever"), or the esoteric moment within every moment of exo-
> teric time. The ultimate self of man, the spirit, resides in God, and
> thus esoteric time. The great mistake of many modern thinkers, says
> Huston Smith, is to deny Aevertinal and to introduce development
> into God, who in ways is made out to be "not yet." Schuon agrees:
> the purely evolutionist view, he says, denies the *constant* "periphery-
> centre relationship."[3]

That esoteric moment dwelling within exoteric time is where time
and eternity collapse upon themselves into one. As I mentioned earlier,
the Scholastic philosophy of the aeviternitas or aeviternity (spelled as
Aevertinity in the above quote) describes a state of consciousness that
an individual experiences where time and eternity are one.

So the spiritual dilemma is that the majority of people are caught
in the linear evolutionary process of time, and opposite this, those
sincere in their own introspection are trying to fix their perception
in eternity. But both are missing the point that samsara and nirvana
are one. The path of initiation reflects this paradox, because an individual begins to slowly grow and learn along the path but consciously
delays enlightenment due to an intellectual desire for more knowledge.
But the knowledge one attains lacks the coherence to allow what has
already been attained to be fully assimilated. The initiatory path works
on the physical and mental planes intensely, but in most cases the process loses sight of the divine ground of the spiritual plane. On the physical plane we begin to take care of the body with much more respect,
and on the mental plane our emotions, feelings, and thoughts become
more pure as we understand our psychology with more clarity. This is

a grand unfoldment on the individual's part, but it is all fundamentally hindered if the perception of the spiritual plane has not come to bear fruit.

This subject matter is thoroughly discussed and known as "the evolution of perception" in my book, *The Science and Practice of Humility*. This state of perception is the awareness Chuang-tzu had of the infinite in all "things," which he called "the still-point of the *Tao*." The great Indian sage Patañjali, who was the father of yoga, called this state of perception "pure awareness," known as *purusha* in Sanskrit (पुरुष). Pure awareness is the root of our consciousness, which is the main principle aspect of the spiritual plane of consciousness. Patañjali believes that the evolutionary aspect of the mind, *citta* in Sanskrit, is to refine the mind back into its original state of pure perception, which reveals that unity within our inner being and outer world. Chip Hartranft dives deep into the wisdom of Patañjali concerning pure awareness in his commentary on the *Yoga-Sūtra of Patañjali*. Hartranft states:

> The aspect that Patañjali calls consciousness, or *citta*, is evolving. Its evolutionary goal is to refine itself to the point where it can become so still, unmoving, and equally absorbed in all phenomena that it becomes very much like pure awareness itself. In that instant, it can reflect pure awareness back to itself, making it realize that it is distinct and separate from nature. . . .
>
> Pure awareness, he insists, is actually not a part of ever changing nature; instead, it is immaterial, unchanging, incorruptible *seeing itself* and merely observes nature operating before it. . . . Pure awareness is the knower of all sights, sounds, smells, tastes, contacts, and thoughts, yet is not *of* them.
>
> Consciousness (*citta*), on the other hand, is the stuff they are made of. Like a television picture, consciousness arises from nature both subtle and gross. It is dependent on the conditions that created and maintain it, and utterly unable to observe itself. . . .

Patañjali states from the outset that pure awareness is overshadowed by the modulations of consciousness, which is continually transformed from one pattern of thought to another and rarely sits still for long. This characteristic of consciousness requires deliberate, consistent, and intensive inner work, or yoking, if one is to awaken from its automaticity and see through its incessant, limiting definitions of reality. . . .

As the senses spontaneously cease to react to external stimuli, a phenomenon Patañjali calls *pratyahara*, consciousness begins to grow calmer and more refined in its perceptions, and capable of noticing the ordinarily invisible movements of consciousness itself. The experience is something like viewing a realistic image in a painting at the far end of a gallery. As one comes closer, the brushstrokes and the texture of the canvas become visible—eventually to the point where the image has completely deconstructed and can no longer be seen unless one elects to step back.[4]

The spiritual seeker and esoteric student are usually handicapped by this tendency to have their perception caught in the detail of life because they cannot perceive the harmony and unity of the world that is before them, as William Blake illuminates in his epic poem *Auguries of Innocence*:

> *To see a World in a Grain of Sand*
> *And a Heaven in a Wild Flower*
> *Hold Infinity in the palm of your hand*
> *And Eternity in an hour*[5]

Only those who dwell on the spiritual plane can step back, as Patañjali suggests, and become aware of the invisible movements of consciousness. The secret societies, mystery schools, and wisdom traditions that promote an initiatory path also promote higher initiates being more attracted to worldly affairs and the status of intellectual prestige and moral intelligence than to the movements of consciousness. Their view of initiation has more to do with creating upright citizens than anything to do with enlightenment. These paths of initiation become a haven for spiritual one-upsmanship, as people within the confines of a sect begin a process of trying to be more knowledgeable, benevolent, and righteous than another.

Initiation loses its spirituality because it is purely a time-bound system, a process of constructing rather than deconstructing intellectual barriers. A thirty-third-degree initiate of Scottish Rite Freemasonry, for example, does not dwell within the pure awareness at the root of consciousness in the same way that a true mystic living in the Wudang Mountains of China, the holy hill of Arunachala in India, or the quietude in a hermitage deep in the forests of Bhutan experience purusha. The thirty-third-degree Freemason has no real connection with pure awareness because his life is continually busy with daily affairs that really differ only slightly from those of the "average Joe." According to the Freemason's contrived system of initiation, enlightenment is not our eternal center of consciousness, but rather, it is an intellectual position of authority that we achieve within "time." Built on a time-bound philosophy, the initiatory path loses the objective of its very nature, which is to reveal enlightenment at the depth of our being.

When it comes to enlightenment, we are always sent out on an adventure, no matter whether it is the path of initiation or by a spiritual guru, to seek the goal and destination of enlightenment. These teachers and methods who perpetuate this belief are doing nothing more than postponing your enlightenment. From the ground of pure awareness it would be absurd to take a journey to the farthest extreme to arrive at where you were originally. This is the paradox of the path of initiation, because in some cases it can blunt the sharpness of the intellect into the awareness that what we seek we already are. Author and scholar Peter Kingsley articulates this initiatory journey to where we already are: "The initiatory journey leads 'far away from the beaten track of humans,' into what can sometimes seem unbearable darkness and isolation. But the journey eventually brings us back to exactly where we began. Nothing new is found that wasn't already present all along."[6]

The path of initiation that developed in ancient times in response to agrarian cultures is an audacious attempt to induce the enlightenment we innately possess. What is not emphasized, and has been essentially lost from the ancient schools of initiation up to the present-day schools of wisdom, is that the path of initiation is a tool for finding discipline taught as an intermediary objective on the way toward acquiring the real esoteric truth, that the goal has always been here and now. Anything in the realm of time will be swallowed up by the limitations of time, except for the timeless pure awareness that an initiatory path is supposed to induce. Patañjali and other exalted masters suggest that there is an initiation of sorts into purusha, or pure awareness. But the kind of initiation they point to has nothing to do with the practice of rites, rituals, and sacrifice. It is rather a refinement of consciousness into the mystical union with the Divine, which takes our perception of reality into the occult initiation of enlightenment.

3
The Occult Initiation of Purusha (Pure Awareness)

IN THE DEEPER RECESSES of consciousness lay dormant *purusha*, pure awareness. Purusha should not be thought of as a consciousness that we acquire or induce over time, because pure awareness is what always exists as the foundation of our consciousness, yet it is invariably veiled by the constant turbulence of mental activity. We commonly believe purusha exists as a phantom of consciousness that only a few sages experience. This of course is discerned within the limitations of mental conditioning, so in reality it is not a true statement regarding pure awareness. The wisdom traditions explain that we are attempting to explore purusha through the limitation of our mind's contents. This is an absurd attempt because, as most wisdom traditions articulate, the contents of mind are the accumulation of experiences that veil purusha, pure awareness.

The dirt that veils the transparency of a window is not the window, but instead an accumulation of dust particles over time. The dirt only seems to be a part of the window for a certain amount of time. In much the same way, our accumulated personality is not pure awareness, as our personality is only an extension and outgrowth of purusha for a limited time, which we call our lifetime. The idea here is not to cast aside your mind activity like a cheap suit, but instead understand your personality more intimately because this will be the stepping-stone on the way back to the mind's foundation of pure awareness. It is more a process of refinement and deepening rather than cleaning out the closet. A sage would advocate a sincere introspection of your entire being, which ultimately allows for the egocentric mind to soften and marinate in the heart of pure awareness.

In Sanskrit the stilling process of the mind is known as *nirodha* (निरोध). This was a teaching employed by such sages as Gautama the Buddha and Patañjali to show their disciples that the nature of mind and nature itself are intrinsically still like water. Water's nature is transparent and reflective until it is disturbed, and this is the nature of pure awareness in relation to the vibrations of mind activity. There's nothing wrong with mind activity, as it is also a natural function of the vital force flowing through our body. But what we need to understand is that our connection with our original state of purusha has been severed by the misunderstanding that the contents of our consciousness are "us." The mystery schools of antiquity understood this, but over the course of history our search for this pure state of consciousness became more outwardly superficial rather than anything inwardly deep. It became this way through the superficial initiatory path, which is subtly built upon the monarchical view of reality.

Those religions, secret societies, mystery schools, and esoteric sects who follow the methodology of initiation lose sight of the initiatory path's objective, which is to experience that nondual state of purusha. The common perception of initiation is of rites, rituals, sacrifice, and obedience to a particular doctrine, and it is more about creating upright and noble people—men usually—rather than achieving complete liberation and realization of one's own pure awareness. As we have already mentioned, this superficial realm of initiation cannot escape the clutches of the monarchical view of reality. Its initiatory process is always based on an ascension through degrees, levels, and layers of understanding that are invariably more intellectual than any intuitive sense of knowing. The esoteric heart of how initiation was originally conceived is beyond anything of physical or mental value, as it is a process and refinement of consciousness from the mundane awareness of matter into the unified awareness of spirit within the world of form. Most of what is called "initiation" fails in this regard.

PERCEPTUAL INITIATION

The original conception of the initiatory process was not anything related to the monarchical view of reality. Its primary basis was rooted in how to realize or cultivate a living experience of pure awareness. This was significant because it is only through an experience of pure awareness that we can discover that sense of unity that all human beings consciously or unconsciously yearn for.

The true initiation is more mysteriously occult than any sort of path or process that we follow superficially. It is occult because the original initiation of the ancient adepts was related to the direct perception of the individual, rather than the indirect perception given to the individual by collective society. The occult and original initiation is how the individual's perception evolves from the so-called dualistic world of form, which is within the physical and mental planes, to the perception of the nondual formlessness from the vantage point of the spiritual plane of consciousness. The perception attained within the spiritual plane of consciousness can intuitively perceive the interconnectedness within the mental and physical planes. What we generally perceive as duality in reality is, from a more subtle level of awareness, perceived as a unified continuation of one energy and consciousness.

The mystics call this perceptual initiation a journey "from matter to consciousness," or "from matter to spirit." If one's perception is in the tranquility of the spiritual plane, one can perceive the harmonious pattern of unity in life through what many people perceive as chaos. That harmonious pattern of unity is perceived because the sense of unity within an individual's consciousness has flowered into the pure awareness of purusha. The union with the irreducible essence that many people seek is a state of consciousness we experience, which is the divine ground of our being, purusha. We cannot really dissect and study pure awareness in the same way that we cannot intellectually study God. But we can feel the experience of purusha, which is the yoga, or union, with God. In Greek this union is known as *gnosis*, experiential knowledge of the Divine. Purusha, being the state of perception of the spiritual plane, is a glimpse of eternity through the looking glass of time. Perceiving the formlessness of eternity in the finite realm of time, as Chuang-tzu did, is an occult initiation that the individual goes through, progressing from their own sense of separation on to their latent sense of divinity. American Rosicrucianist Reuben Swinburne Clymer explains this aspect of occult initiation: "Occult initiation is not to be confused with ordinary ceremonial initiation, however beautifully illustrative it may be. Occult initiation is the gradual revelation of the Mysteries to the Soul as it gains interior *Consciousness* of its Divinity or Immortality."[1]

This perceptual initiation should not be confused with the monarchical view of the universe, because this perception is neither high nor low and does not relate to the world of time. In the contemplative texts this perception of pure awareness is thought of generally as a higher state in the monarchical sense, because it is the evolved perception within the spiritual plane. Yet, this view is too compartmentalized, as it attempts to dissect and segregate the physical, mental, and spiritual planes of consciousness from each other. This outlook results from the monarchical view, as many people assume these planes are layers of attainment, rather than one singular process of consciousness experienced by different individuals differently. To assume that the physical, mental, and spiritual are separate indicates that we have overlooked the principles that allow the universe and consciousness to mutually arise. Hermetic philosophy best describes these principles, particularly the first three principles of seven passed down by Hermes Trismegistus. The first three principles state:

I. THE PRINCIPLE OF MENTALISM
THE ALL is MIND; The Universe is Mental.

II. THE PRINCIPLE OF CORRESPONDENCE
As above, so below; as below, so above.

III. THE PRINCIPLE OF VIBRATION
Nothing rests; everything moves; everything vibrates.[2]

The Principle of Mentalism should not be confused with the mind as we know it, because the terminology of old is different from that of the modern era. So when Hermes states that "THE ALL is MIND; The Universe is Mental," he means that "Everything is Consciousness; The Universe is Consciousness." American occultist William Walker Atkinson, writing under the pseudonym of the "Three Initiates," sheds light on this within his Hermetic classic, *The Kybalion: Hermetic Philosophy:*

> This Principle embodies the truth that "All is Mind." It explains that THE ALL (which is the Substantial Reality underlying all the outward manifestations and appearances which we know under the terms of "The Material Universe"; the "Phenomena of Life"; "Matter"; "Energy"; and, in short, all that is apparent to our material senses) is SPIRIT, which in itself is UNKNOWABLE and UNDEFINABLE, but which may be considered and thought of as AN UNIVERSAL, INFINITE, LIVING MIND.[3]

This understanding that All is consciousness, or to use Atkinson's word, "spirit," is not limited to Hermeticism, but also builds the foundation of many religious and spiritual paths, including Buddhism, Hinduism, Gnosticism, and Taoism. This understanding is also examined through the lens of modern science, particularly quantum physics and the holographic model. Pure awareness resides eternally within the foundation of this all pervasive consciousness known as the spiritual plane within the ancient wisdom traditions. This is why the Principle of Correspondence means that everything is consciousness, because within the physical planes of consciousness exists also the mental and spiritual planes, and vice versa. Hence "As above, so below; as below, so above." This is surely only one aspect of this ancient Hermetic axiom, but it gives us a deeper explanation of how the physical, mental, and spiritual planes are not in some order of monarchy, as the world of matter and spirit are the mutual outcome of propagations of vibration, which brings us to the Principle of Vibration. Yet, this dance of energy that we call vibration is not a complete picture without the fifth principle of Hermeticism:

V. THE PRINCIPLE OF RHYTHM

Everything flows, out and in; everything has its tides; all things rise and fall; the pendulum-swing manifests in everything; the measure of the swing to the right is the measure of the swing to the left; rhythm compensates.[4]

Vibration and rhythm, as I discuss at length within my book *The Science and Practice of Humility,* constitutes on a very subtle level the magnification of our individual perception. In relation to the musical scale the higher the octave the finer the vibration. Yet, as we know, what is perceived as higher in the scale of music is not considered higher from a monarchical standpoint. Each octave actually depends on the other, no matter whether we perceive it as low or high, because it is the harmony of all octaves that constitutes rhythm.

The occult initiation of purusha in the wisdom traditions is the ability to perceive this rhythm within reality. This is done by our perception ascending the scale of consciousness in much the same way as the musical scale, onto that higher and finer vibration of pure awareness. Purusha is the perception that can sincerely become conscious of a vibratory and rhythmic order within the world of chaotic form. The perception that is caught in the chaotic details of the physical and mental planes is not any different or in opposition to the perception that is focused on the spiritual plane. We could say that they are poles apart, but not different, as the act of perceiving is a rhythm comparable to that of breathing. In Hinduism this rhythmic process is known as the "breath of Brahma," and in occult tradition as the "involution and evolution of perception and consciousness."

The physical, mental, and spiritual planes act according to the rhythmic process, as matter and spirit are held together by the vibration and rhythm intrinsic within consciousness. Metaphysics—the science of the physical, mental and spiritual planes of consciousness tells us, "All is consciousness."

We only assume that matter and spirit are separate according to our social, cultural, and religious indoctrination of the monarchical view. The superficial aspects of religion tend to believe that spirit *influences* matter because spirit and matter are perceived to be separate, just like the equally false idea that the individual and the universe/God are separate. Those who are imprisoned by religious dogma usually never wonder how we could have ever conceived of God from being within the world of matter. Consciousness and the way we perceive reality, which both gave rise to the original concept of God, are somehow left outside dogmatic religious beliefs and speculation, because to explore the inner world goes against the monarchical view of reality. To be one with God, as most religious beliefs claim to seek, is to be sincere in one's introspection, which elevates one's perception into the mysterious occult initiation.

In the occult initiation of our perception, we become ever more conscious that matter and spirit cannot be separate, as the physical plane is not lower than the mental and spiritual planes. Rather, all three planes are instead a flux of energy consisting of all the principles of eternity within the world of form. In the pure awareness of purusha the axiomatic truth that "the universe produces consciousness and consciousness evokes the universe" is known beyond the limitations of words. But a state of perception caught within the clutches of *prakrti* (प्रकृति, Sanskrit for the endless motion of the phenomenal world), tends to get lost in the intellectual meanings of words, rather than perceiving their true, symbolic meaning. The misinterpretation of spiritual texts, methods, and the occult initiation of perception, have all come at the hands of those people who were still enslaved by the monarchical view. The idea of a multilayered initiation was not only subject to perception and the way we perceive matter and spirit, but also infiltrated the very steps most of us take to cultivate the pure awareness of purusha.

A CLASSIFICATION OF DEPTH METAPHYSICS AND SPIRITUAL WISDOM

The superficial initiatory path has plagiarized some of the most profound wisdom of many spiritual traditions, especially in the wisdom from places such as China and India. The New Age understandings of yoga, t'ai chi, qi, the chakra system, and so on, are totally disconnected from the deeper aspects of such knowledge. The majority of New Age gurus and followers have a tendency to over-sensationalize such knowledge, which as a result becomes more "spacy" than grounded. The New Age pop spirituality is completely intellectual with no true sense of self, as those influenced by such spacy philosophy only parrot aphorisms in a condescending tone, which is a direct result of the hypnosis of the monarchical view of reality. For example, if someone is having some challenging psychological problem, a New Ager may parrot "It's all an illusion" or "Everything is harmony," which is a totally inappropriate response, and only intellectual rather than actually spiritual, because if they truly knew that all is an illusion and harmonious then there should be no problem in tending to the heartache of another.

People bound by New Age understandings of spirituality lack a real "knowing" of what the ego and intellect are, as they continue to be lost superficially in words in a constant game of spiritual one-upmanship.

Real, honest self-work is ignored within the New Age because the intellectual repetition of profound words disguises their ignorance with the idea that they are somehow enlightened beings on a plane of beautiful light, higher than the rest of us. Again, this implies a lack of real self-work, because when we become truly sincere in our own introspection, what we discover about ourselves can be quite gruesome, especially when we explore our repressed pain.

THE CHAKRAS: THE PSYCHOLOGICAL CENTERS

Many people in the New Age fall into the trap, either from their guru or by misinterpretation of wisdom, into believing that they are enlightened beings sent here to save humanity from their hypnosis. This may appear grand to some, but to believe of yourself in this way is a subtle effect of the monarchical view and a messiah complex. Our systems of spiritual wisdom and metaphysics are over-sensationalized and tampered with as a result of such monarchical thinking. The energetic chakra system of Hinduism (see figure 3.1), and the yogic paths are a good indication of such misinterpreted manipulation of knowledge.

The chakra system is based on seven centers of energy condensed within the human body. According to the texts of the tantric tradition there are many chakras in the subtle human body, but there are seven main chakras that build the foundation of this system of knowledge. The seven chakras in Sanskrit are *sahasrara* (crown chakra), *ajna* (third eye chakra), *vishuddha* (throat chakra), *anahata* (heart chakra), *manipura* (solar plexus chakra), *swadhisthana* (sacral chakra), and *muladhara* (root chakra). *Chakra* in Sanskrit means "wheel" or "turning" of energy, and in a yogic context it refers to a "vortex" or "whirlpool" of energy.

A problem with the general understanding of the chakra system arises in how we perceive energy and the seven centers. The common misunderstanding, especially in the New Age, is that the seven centers are laid out one above the other within the subtle body of a human,

Figure 3.1. The Seven Energetic Chakra Systems
Illustration by Daniel A. Stewart

and are thought of to be totally disconnected from one another in a fashion that each and every individual resides on different chakras without feeling the effects of the chakras they believe they have transcended. This idea of separation of chakras, a layered perception of chakras, and a step-by-step approach to healing them is a direct result of the monarchical view. In this view, we strive to isolate ourselves on an illusionary spiritual abode above the rest. We discount many factors in this narrow view of the chakra system.

For example, the chakras in original Hindu philosophy have a direct relationship to the psychophysical constitution of the human body found in the Indian science of health known as Ayurveda. In this context, the chakras are thought of as "temperaments" that we go through in relation to the constitution of the physical and mental planes of the individual and the energy we transform from the five elements that are known in Ayurveda as the three *doshas*, or the Tridosha Theory, called *vata, pitta,* and *kapha* (see figure 3.2).

When we truly explore such Hindu systems such as the chakras and Ayurveda it exposes our modern tendency to attempt to make

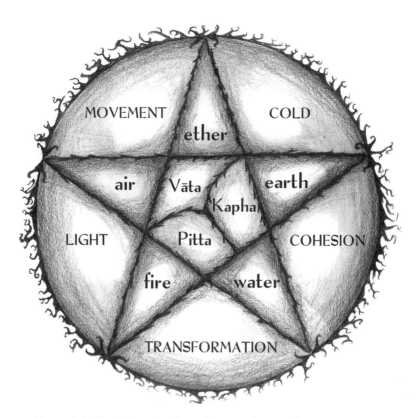

Figure 3.2. The Three Doshas of Ayurveda and the Five Elements
Illustration by Daniel A. Stewart

conclusions without completely assimilating the knowledge on offer. Our monarchical conclusions about chakras arise from the other problem mentioned earlier, the way we perceive energy. In New Age circles energy is an "airy fairy" concept, lacking any real foundation. People express their relationship to a chakra center of energy through empty proclamations, such as "Look out! I'm opening my heart chakra." The general awareness of energy is misunderstood.

In relation to the Hindu chakra system we need to understand that there is a vital force of energy flowing through our body that is comparable, if not exactly the same, to electricity. Our neural network, nervous system, and meridians are the carriers of this electricity, known in Sanskrit as *prana* and in Chinese as *qi*. Examining this vital force, a human being is analogous to a light bulb, because electricity illuminates the light bulb in the same way that the vital force of the nervous system illuminates the mind and psychological functions. The spike of energy within the human being condenses into our brain and emanates as our activity of mind and basic psychology. According to Ayurveda, our complete nervous system draws in the experience of life through our senses, and this is the energy that is supplied to our brain and becomes mental activity. Austrian philosopher, social reformer, architect, and esotericist Rudolf Steiner elaborates upon this by explaining that the human being is an upside down tree, because qi flows through the nervous system into the neural network of the brain as mind activity. The original understanding of energy in relation to the human body is an intelligence we all possess in our bodies, psychologies, body movements, and organ functions.

The energetic chakras are, as American mythologist Joseph Campbell explained, psychological centers. The chakras have a definitive essence that drives our emotional habits and tendencies. Campbell explains the psychological characteristics as the dormant feminine energy at the base of our spine (*kundalini* in Sanskrit) rises through the first three chakras (using *lotus* as another name for chakra, and spelling *chakra* as *cakra*):

The first lotus is called *muladhara,* which means "root base." At this lotus, the serpent is coiled up and inert in its lair at the base of the spine. At this point the serpent is like a dragon. We all know the character of dragons—at least, Western dragons: they live in caves, and they have a gold hoard in the cave, and they have a beautiful girl whom they have captured in the cave. They can't do anything with either treasure or maiden, but they simply want *to hold on.* Dragons, like people whose lives are centered around the first *cakra,* are based around gripping, holding on to power, holding on to a life that is no life at all because there is no animation in it, no joy in it, no vitality in it, but just grim, dogged existence. The nature of the *kundalini* at *muladhara* is that of Ebenezer Scrooge before he undergoes that grand journey and transformation at the hands of the three ghosts in Charles Dickens's *A Christmas Carol.*

The second *cakra* is at the level of the genitalia and is called *svadhishthana,* which means "her favorite resort." This is the *cakra* that centers itself entirely around the experience of pleasure, or *kama.* When one's spiritual energy is operating on this level, one's psychology is completely Freudian. Sex is the only aim; sex is the great frustration.

When the *kundalini* moves up again, it reaches the level of the navel or stomach. This *cakra* is called *manipura,* which means "the city of the shining jewel." Here the interest is in consuming everything, being master of everything, eating everything, turning it into your own substance; this is, after all, the *cakra* of the belly. When the energy is at this level, one's psychology is completely Nietzschean or Alderian. One wants to consume and gain power for oneself over everything; one is driven by a will to power. This is the level at which the *artha* principle, the drive to succeed, is centered.[5]

The term for the fourth chakra, within the heart, *anahata* means "not hit." This refers to a sound, but not the kind that is made by two things striking together. This is reminiscent of the Zen koan "What is the sound of one hand clapping?" All sounds we hear are made by two or more things striking or having friction with one another. The sound that comes from somewhere other than two things striking together is the sound of Brahman, the primordial *aum* (in Sanskrit om, ॐ). Indians often say that to get an understanding of aum one should cover one's ears and listen. The sound of Brahman, aum (om), is the energy of which the world is a precipitation. At the heart chakra one begins to sense the faculty that aum is within all things, which is the sense of unity I have referred to before. Yet the sound is not so much something you hear, but instead it is a silence you sense in the interconnected hum of life. This may seem paradoxical, to equate the sound of aum with silence, but aum is often thought to have four syllables rather than three. The fourth syllable in this three syllable word is the silence that exists before the sound and after the sound. However, in the manifest world aum is still the result of matter and spirit striking a chord together. But the intrinsic nature of aum is its silence. This relationship between aum and silence is discovered when we chant a mantra repetitively. When we say aum it is still two things striking together (that is, air molecules being struck by our vibrating vocal cords), but when we continue to chant a mantra our mind moves into a state of silence where the unity of life is a reality. This silence allows our awareness to hear aum in all things. As a result, our inner being moves away from the focus that drives the first three chakras.

The fifth chakra, at the level of the larynx, vishuddha is the purging of all *vasanas* (habitual ways and latent tendencies) that obscure our connection to the sound of Brahman. This is a moving inward to sincere self-work. It is a purification of our perception, in which we seek to move through all limitations of duality and into the nondual awareness.

At the sixth chakra, ajna, we become the bridge between heaven and earth. The yin (earth/feminine/passive/receptive/coolant) and yang (heaven/masculine/active/creative/heat) archetypes of the psyche celebrate an alchemical marriage. The soul has found its true love for the universal beloved. This love extends to all life, since the relationship to the universal beloved is experienced through everybody and everything. This is the consciousness of a holy sage.

The seventh chakra, sahasrara, is the mystical abode where the subject-object split disappears. A difference between soul and the irreducible essence (universal beloved) dissolves. From a purely psychological perspective it is difficult to talk about this state because it transcends all ideas of relationship and duality itself.

Although the chakras include a first to a seventh, deepening our connection to them is not a sequential process as, for example, the 33-step initiation process of the Freemasons is. Ascending the chakras is an inner process, opposed to initiation processes that are imposed on one from the outside, and the progression is not black and white. We may move from first to seventh, or we may begin our internal work at any point in between. We all have all seven chakras, but each chakra is activated based on where we place our awareness. So if you are operating from a dominator mindset based on power, control, force, for example, then you reside in the lower three chakras, but that doesn't mean the seventh chakra doesn't exist or is not mutual with the lower three. Likewise, if you are operating from a state of consciousness focused on unconditional love, compassion, forgiveness, humility, peaceful silence, and a sincere effort to transcend your ego's notion of its own self-centered importance and its latent conditioning that fuels this belief, then you reside in the fourth, fifth, and sixth chakras. However, if we become imbalanced in one of our lower chakras, we may have to return our attention to that chakra, finding balance there in order to return to an awareness filled with the qualities of the upper chakras. Residing in these upper chakras opens the mysterious doorway of the seventh chakra, a state of consciousness we can hardly fathom or speak about. All that can be said about the seventh chakra is that it is a nondual reality devoid of the subject-object split, as experienced by an authentic mystic, where there is no separation at all within their pure consciousness.

THE PSYCHOLOGY OF TAOIST ENERGY

The ancient knowledge of psychological centers of energy also appears in Chinese Taoism. In Taoism energy is thought of as all the experiential information we take in through our nervous system, that is, the nine gates that either promote or hinder our psychological growth.* Taoist practices include techniques to purge the accumulated toxic energy that hinders our growth. Similar to the chakra system, the psychological centers are discovered through the intelligence of the body. We have the intelligence of the "gut," or "gut instinct," known by the Chinese as the *lower dantien*, which is in constant dialogue with the *middle dantien* located at the level of the heart, and the *upper dantien* located in the pineal gland of the brain and commonly known as the "third eye." In qigong and Traditional Chinese Medicine (TCM) the upper, middle, and lower dantien are not separate or layered, but instead they are mutual and depend on each other for a human being to have an experience of life.

The chakras or the dantien might be perceived as arbitrary layers or steps, but in this the concept of layers is again misinterpreted and lost in translation. In the esoteric and wisdom traditions, layers and levels refer to one's psychological ability to interpret life. This relates to the occult initiation of perception and the virtue of an individual who can perceive reality from the spiritual plane of consciousness. If we are to completely understand that consciousness exists in three planes—physical, mental, and spiritual—then our psychological ability to interpret life with clarity depends on our psychophysical constitution. Indian spiritual guru Swami Satchidananda said:

> It's very simple. Keep your body as clean as possible, your mind as clear as possible. That's all you need. And do it in any way you

---

*The nine gates in esoteric wisdom are the two eyes, two ears, two nostrils, mouth, anus, and penis or vagina.

can, in your own way. It doesn't matter. That's why I say "peaceful body, peaceful mind." And then you'll be useful. You don't have to become a useful person. You will be useful.[6]

This is not to say that an individual dwelling on the lower chakras cannot have a peak experience or experience nirvana. Anyone can attain such states because nirvana is latent within us. But what is being said here is that the likelihood of having a sustained peak experience or feeling of the blissful nirvana is minimal if we are not in healthy balance between the physical, mental, and spiritual planes of consciousness. All of our misconceptions and false conclusions arise from individuals who are not sincere in their own self-work, and as a result, their psychological ability to interpret life is obscured. Purusha, pure awareness, is the ability to interpret life as it truly *is,* which facilitates the experience of nirvana or the Sanskrit *samadhi* (समाधि). Yet, as the majority of people have never had the experience of purusha, we tend to think of nirvana and enlightenment in association with an event or perfection. The instruments of time, especially the initiatory path and the monarchical view, make us assume that the end of our spiritual struggle through life is the equanimity of purusha and illumination of enlightenment, as if they are an event in the making. How could our innate perception and natural state of consciousness be something we celebrate in the future?

4
The Imperfection and Nonevent of Enlightenment

INGRAINED INTO OUR CULTURE is the belief that we should continually strive to reach a point of perfection in our life somewhere off in the distant future. From childhood we are taught, by both our parents and the educational system, that we should always struggle to reach our goals, which are invariably far off into the distant future. Yet let's be mindful here that there is nothing inherently wrong with setting goals and directing our focus into that desired direction. Without our goals and focus nothing in our world—good or bad—could manifest because in most cases when one achieves a goal it has the ability to inspire. So setting goals and directing our focus to achieve these goals are not the problem; the real problem of this ingrained cultural struggle is to believe that once we arrive at our goals we will somehow experience a state of contentment or happiness, which is supposed to signify perfection.

Though this is the social template for experiencing perfection, many people on their deathbed have a deep sense of emptiness and bewilderment because they finally realize that their whole life was wasted chasing a concept of perfection that never came. A lot of people incorrectly blame themselves on their deathbed for not reaching what they had perceived as perfection. This is tremendously sad, considering that what many people associate perfection with is along the narrow social and cultural lines of success. We allow ourselves to be caught in the details of these social and cultural notions of success. But when we reflect upon our life before passing into the unknowable, we lose sight of what really mattered in our life.

From greater clarity and an elevated perception, we can see that what really matters in our life is what many people take for granted and overlook: those elements of our life that bring balance and joy into consciousness. What really matters in our life are the people we share our love with and who love us in return; the joy of learning from each other, especially the subtle things about ourselves; growing more into a state of unmoving love, compassion, and forgiveness outside the scope of what many people perceive as perfection. Our perception is so lost in the details of life that we discount what we already have in our life, and so we somehow assume that this wonderful life we are already living is not perfection. The simple things in life are generally overlooked. It is usually only when we experience the grief of losing a loved one that we realize the simple things are the most important and intrinsically perfect aspects of our lives.

The fundamental basis of human life—relationships—is often thought of more as a hindrance in everyday life because if someone contradicts our concrete idea of reality then we attempt to edit them out of our life. We have no foresight to recognize how most of our beliefs are limited and always open to change. Confused by our beliefs, which are borrowed from society, culture, and religion, we define and categorize perfection in association with who we believe we should be in the future. Yet when that moment comes to fruition we never experience it fully because we are already off in the dreamworld of the future, chasing more so-called success and another version of ourselves more perfect than who we are in the here and now. Our culture is built on an idea of life in the future, which has the masses working incessantly toward these "goals." But these goals are never absolute, and they change and morph in relation to what is important in the present moment.

When our striving fails we always come back to what is needed right now. All of our ecological problems result from this future striving for an ideal world, which is usually only ideal to the banks, corporations, religions, and governments who fund such a vain imagination. In our quest to achieve this so-called ideal world (invariably ideal only from a Western perspective), we strip nature bare with our excessive greed. Our insatiable thirst for energy resources reflects this greed, as we see with the mining and deforestation industries, the rape of Mother Earth so we can have our comforts and convenience, which are supposed to result in a perfect world. The social, cultural, and religious notion of perfection is destroying our planet and hypnotizing humanity into a zombified sleep state. This game we play with nature results from the monarchical view, because we are attempting to be nature's lord, both directly and indirectly. The problem with this battle we are locked into with nature is that we will lose, not because we are weak or unintelligent, but because of the most obvious fact that many people overlook: we *are* nature.

To destroy our planet is to destroy humanity, and the earth will move on and cleanse itself after we are gone, as the late great comedian George Carlin emphasized, "The planet will be here for a long, long, LONG time after we're gone, and it will heal itself, it will cleanse itself, 'cause that's what it does. It's a self-correcting system. The air and the water will recover, the earth will be renewed."[1]

The perfection we and the world strive for in our life does nothing but destroy the individual and the world. The moment of success we are supposed to achieve around the age of forty, after all of our schooling, college, and struggle up the ladder of work and prestige results only in a deep feeling of emptiness, because we realize that we possess only fool's gold rather than the real thing. We finally understand that we were cheated and robbed of our experience of being a vibrant youth.

We constantly have our eye on the destination and pay no attention to the journey. The destination is thought of as perfection, as if we are not perfectly all right as we are right now. We destroy ourselves individually and collectively as a result of this notion of success in relation to perfection. When we feel cheated from our journey and experience emptiness, we seek new destinations and set new goals to fill this empty void in our life. We sometimes seek a way out of life by any means necessary because we falsely believe we are inadequate in the eyes of others who appear happy and successful. People often strive to be like celebrities without realizing that they too are human with their own problems and delusions of perfection. When all else fails people turn to religion because they believe their narrow idea of God (or Krishna, Lao-tzu, Buddha, Jesus, Muhammad) must be a surefire way to perfection.

Yet if we can bring some sanity to the topic—which will conflict with most religious fundamentalists, who are out of sync with God—if such religious figures, such as Lao-tzu, Buddha, Jesus, and Muhammad, really were human instead of mythological or allegorical expressions then they too had to experience all the ups and downs that human life entails. Believing these religious figures to have a monopoly on enlightenment (that is, Jesus as the "only" son of God, or Muhammad as God's "only" prophet) puts these figures in the monarchical position of a king, and thus excludes the possibility of our own individual enlightenment, disconnecting us from God in a realm of perpetual suffering. Obviously, those not imprisoned by intellectual dogma can clearly perceive that enlightenment is a state of consciousness we can all experience. But it has nothing to do with any supernatural realm filled with anthropomorphic angels, demons, or gods.

Zen Buddhism can bring some clarity to our vain imaginings:

> *Before enlightenment*
> *chopping wood*
> *carrying water.*

> *After enlightenment*
> *chopping wood*
> *carrying water.*[2]

This Zen proverb does not categorize enlightenment as some glorious state, but instead a moment in our lives when we come to our senses about our own hypnosis, and yet in this moment there still is the realization that life goes on. In a moment like this one is finally drawn to authentic spirituality, meaning the inner introspection and outer understanding beyond the doctrinal prisons of organized religion. But even though people are drawn to their own innate spirituality, the social and cultural idea of striving for perfection still persists. In this case we project our idea of perfection onto enlightenment as a goal to be reached.

Perfection becomes a problematic aspect of our life regarding our spirituality and enlightenment. We are still missing the depth of simplicity in this Zen proverb. Our minds are clouded by the thirst for perfection. This monarchical model of perfection is never achieved, so why do we perpetually fall prey to its influence? Just as many people never question the monarchical view, they also never question continually striving for success and perfection. Surely the validity of perfection should be up for question if humanity continually suffers from striving for it!

PERFECTION IS BOUND TO TIME

Our view of perfection is totally disconnected from the present moment. Perfection stands as an illumined mirage within the desert of our mind. We feel that it is just on the horizon, so we need to tighten our bootlaces and continue to charge on. But what we learn in life is that this mirage always remains on the horizon no matter how hard we strive to get there. It doesn't matter how many educational degrees you attain or how many social titles you accumulate, perfection still remains a ghost that you will keep chasing until you are worn out. Spiritually we treat enlightenment in the same regard.

A spiritual seeker and esoteric student often thinks of enlightenment as perfection, and so it always remains on the horizon of our consciousness. We take up all sorts of methods and meditation practices in the hopeful promise that these avenues are a surefire way to enlightenment. But we learn over time that they were not what they promised, and so we move hurriedly on to the next method. When you observe the spiritually inclined you can see that this goes on and on. In all cases, whether social, cultural, religious, or spiritual, we have this tendency to assume that we are somehow not already good enough exactly the way we are now. We have this tendency because the basis of worldly thought is always within the context of the monarchical view of reality. So many people are imprisoned by monarchical thinking, as they always assume they are lesser than government, other people, God, and the universe itself.

We always have this false sense of humility, like the unctuousness of Uriah Heep in the Charles Dickens novel *David Copperfield*. But if the monarchical view is a time-bound philosophy, then why should we feel lesser right where we are in the here and now? The concept of perfection makes us feel this sense of worthlessness. And yet, if perfection is within the contextual framework of monarchy, then how we perceive perfection itself must be time-bound. This awareness not only changes the paradigm within the social and cultural spheres, but it also changes our perception of what enlightenment actually *is*.

Enlightenment is the state of consciousness that we all seek to live, either knowingly or unknowingly. A master will expound that this is a state of perfection beyond time and meaning. Though we hear these words, it is hard for most to fathom the profundity of such an explanation, because perfection in our world is thought of as a state we will reach in the future. We cannot fathom it because we continue to seek what we already are. Our awareness is fixed on a linear framework, which eclipses the nonlinear world we know hardly anything about. Enlightenment is a state of consciousness that has deconstructed the limitations of time while still dwelling within time. In this state one brings eternity into manifestation without any desire to do so, as it is a way of being.

Enlightenment is the resonance of eternity within our consciousness, and yet it shines through the time-bound reality but is not of time itself. Sages from ancient and modern times would find it amusing that many people equate enlightenment as a place in time because to them this is like trying to eat a pizza without the actual dough. We would find eating a pizza without the dough foolish; just so, a sage finds the attempt to reach "perfection in time" foolish as well. A sage knows that perfection is a subjective notion that differs from one individual to the next. A sage finds order in chaos, perfection in what many perceive as imperfection, and this order can be revealed only from an elevated state of perception. What we overlook in life, those aspects of life that we judge as imperfect, are exactly what a sage finds beautiful. Imagine having the foreground of Leonardo da Vinci's *Mona Lisa* with no background. Both are mutual and depend on each other. "Without the detail there can be no greater perspective," which is the axiom behind the Vedic principle of the breath of Brahma.

One of the problems with our civilization is we focus only on details with no view of the greater perspective. We separate out the beautiful and discard what we believe is ugly—again from only a subjective and narrow point of view. Lost in the details, we destroy the world because our perception is fogged by the lens of division. Our consciousness of separation excludes much more than we actually perceive.

We edit our reality to suit our own conditioning based on our egocentric pleasures. The "perfection" we all attempt to reach is based on such ignorance. If we ignore aspects of life that conflict with our conditioning, then is this not ignorance? Is not our ignorance imperfect because we are leaving out more of reality than our conditioning can handle? This form of ignorance is how many people, especially in organized religion, attempt to reach that state of perfection known as enlightenment. We can never understand perfection if we do not understand the wisdom of imperfection. Our striving for perfection narrows our perception of reality because we are constantly editing out the background of what makes the foreground beautiful.

The original Taoist sage, Lao-tzu, explains in chapter 2 of the Tao Te Ching that to define and segregate reality distorts reality, which can be understood deeply if we have the coherence to realize that perceived extremes in reality are actually mutually dependent. Lao-tzu poetically states:

> *When people see some things as beautiful,*
> *other things become ugly.*
> *When people see some things as good,*
> *other things become bad.*
>
> *Being and non-being create each other.*
> *Difficult and easy support each other.*
> *Long and short define each other.*
> *High and low depend on each other.*
> *Before and after follow each other.*
>
> *Therefore the Master*
> *acts without doing anything*
> *and teaches without saying anything.*
> *Things arise and she lets them come;*
> *things disappear and she lets them go.*
> *She has but doesn't possess,*
> *acts but doesn't expect.*
> *When her work is done, she forgets it.*
> *That is why it lasts forever.*[3]

Lao-tzu's view of reality is diametrically opposed to the way the majority of people view the world, as the ancient master would deem it absurd to strive for something that exists within the paradox of time and eternity. Lao-tzu, like many other masters, would explain to those searching for enlightenment that true perfection lies within imperfection. Within the imperfection of time lies the perfection of eternity.

Within samsara is nirvana and vice versa. The two are mutual, but are perceived as such only by those with an evolved perception. It is this perception that facilitates evolution and enlightenment within the consciousness of the individual. Yet most of us still chase the shadow of enlightenment in the realm of time.

To see imperfection and perfection as one and the same state has always been a radical view of reality, but it is the only sane understanding, because the way in which we generally perceive perfection in time can be put to the sword and discarded from our world. And the best way to explain this is through our vain strivings for enlightenment. Our modern perspective differs from the wisdom of Lao-tzu in that our idea of "enlightenment" is associated with perfection. Again, the way we perceive perfection has not come under the microscope of critical analysis. Ask yourself, why do you seek enlightenment? It is a strange question to ask because it is intrinsically paradoxical. On the one hand we feel a latent desire to attain enlightenment, while on the other we feel we've been duped into seeking what is originally ours. This paradox leaves us stranded in confusion.

But when our confusion dissipates, the light of awareness shines upon our idea of perfection, revealing its false promises and lack of foundation. Perfection is a contradiction because it pretends to be beyond time, but in fact it is only a notion arising from the realm of time.

No matter how we look at it, conventional ideas of perfection are a product of time. Our searching and striving for perfection in any sphere of life shows it is limited to time. Perfection is what we believe is at the end of the rainbow, but that is unreachable. We think perfection is gold, until we realize it's only fool's gold. Our search for enlightenment leads us to this fool's gold at the end of the rainbow of our own spiritual practice. We feel cheated as a result. But this is not a stab at spiritual practice, as I am also a practitioner of numerous internal arts. Yet we have to come to grips with the fact that our discipline will not induce a state already innate in our being. Spiritual practices may clean out a lot of conditioned garbage from our mind. They may refine our consciousness, and they can clear the clouds of hypnosis, making it easier to finally perceive the clear light of the sun within ourselves. But if we cling to such practices they can become obstacles.

THE PARADOX OF DOING AND NONDOING ASPECTS OF CONSCIOUSNESS

The great sage of India, Patañjali, was particularly interested in the paradox of the "doing" and "nondoing" aspects of consciousness. In relation to yoga he explores how our practice of yoga, or any other spiritual practice for that matter, can eventually be an obstacle standing in front of our liberation. Chip Hartranft lucidly explains this in the introduction to his translation of the *Yoga-Sūtra of Patañjali:*

> In every domain of personhood, therefore, we must make an effort to bring about yogic transformation. However, in Patañjali's view the commotion of our ordinary physical and mental life conceals the fact that our thoughts and actions are almost always tinged with wanting, aversion, egoism, or fear of extinction. Thus, as we settle into the stilling process, or *nirodha,* we come to recognize that these energies of suffering are the sparks quickening every part of our inner landscape into action. This includes even our efforts to transcend them through yoga. No matter how deep our sincerity or robust our desire to awaken, we cannot move very far toward clarity before certain of our efforts themselves become obstacles on our path.[4]

We prevent ourselves from realizing the clear light of enlightenment within our consciousness. The obstacles standing in our way are the attractions we have to the means of our goal rather than the goal itself. We perpetually postpone our enlightenment because of our unrealistic concept that the goal is somehow a state of perfection. We have our eyes fixed on this mirage instead of being conscious of where we are right here and now. From this perspective we separate the destination from the journey. We glamorize the goal or destination, seeing it as blissful and perfect, as if reaching this place in the future will make us eternally content. Yet we understand this is untrue because when people achieve their goal of success they feel no different from the way they did before. When people achieve these goals they finally realize the temporality of the happiness they associated with such goals. The goal was not an event that opened up a gateway of bliss and ecstasy, but instead it was a mere abstraction from the contentment of the journey itself. This also relates to the perfection we project onto the so-called spiritual goal of enlightenment.

SAMADHI IS NO EVENT

When spiritually inclined people hear the words *nirvana, moksha,* or *samadhi,* all sorts of glamorous connotations relating to future perfection pop up in their minds. Beautiful Sanskrit words such as these connote the blissful feeling we attain from enlightenment. But people tend to get distracted by the superficial meaning of such terms, ignoring their deeper connotations. When many people hear the word *samadhi,* for example, they believe it is an event experienced on reaching the goal of enlightenment. This event is often believed to be a plane of light so beautiful that it is beyond the description of words, where we enjoy a Heaven which is more in relation to a psychedelic and trance experience than the original state of Heaven in the here and now. Though the plane of beautiful light may be a great depiction in a Hollywood film or to a New Ager, it is not the reality of samadhi, complete absorption in Atman (the Self/undifferentiated consciousness), enlightenment. Not to shatter any illusions you may have about samadhi, but the reality of such a state is much simpler than one might think. In fact the simplest that you can think of is not even close. In Paramahansa Yogananda's *Autobiography of a Yogi* he explains his daily life and routine with his guru, Swami Sri Yukteswar: "My daily life at the ashram flowed smoothly, infrequently varied. My guru awoke before dawn. Lying down, or sometimes sitting on the bed, he entered a state of *samadhi*."[5]

The state of samadhi Swami Sri Yukteswar entered was not an event like visiting the Moscow Circus, but instead it was a state of equanimity and concentrated stillness of the mind. In Swami Sri Yukteswar's epic *The Holy Science* there are two descriptions of samadhi:

> *Samadhi* is a blissful superconscious state in which a yogi perceives the identity of the individualized soul and Cosmic Spirit.
> *Samadhi*, true concentration, enables one to abandon individuality for universality.[6]

Samadhi is the coalesced contemplation of integration that we enter in meditation. It is more like simple quietude and stillness than any event that you believe is going to save you. These words may appear deflating for those who were hoping that enlightenment was going to save them from their relative life as a human being, but I have no desire for you to join the circus of spiritual misinterpretation. The truth of samadhi is that it is not an event that we will experience in the future, as that perception still constitutes the realm of time.

We project onto *samadhi* and *enlightenment* the idea that we will be saved from our suffering sometime in the future. But our suffering is woven into our relative experience of time, so the perfection we seek at the end of this suffering will continue to be suffering, because it is encased within time. There is nothing actually wrong with our relative experience as a human being, because it's all we know and without it variety would not be the spice of life. Problems with our relativity arise only when we try to escape it rather than accept and embrace it. We have this notion built into the monarchical view that we need to be saved, but what we don't realize in the fog of our own ego-centeredness is that we only need to be saved from ourselves. Ideas of perfection and enlightenment save nobody, as they are incorrectly thought of as events in the future.

But how could enlightenment be an event? How could our individual salvation be isolated to a moment in time when salvation implies eternal liberation? Enlightenment is no event. How could it be if eternity is right here and now? As long as we think of enlightenment as a state of perfection and an event we experience, we will continue to suffer and we will never realize the beautiful perfection and enlightened state of our consciousness in the here and now. Samadhi or enlightenment is in relation to the feeling aspect of the universe, which humans usually refer to as living from the heart. And this intuitive feeling aspect of our consciousness is known when we completely let go of trying to control life, let go of our ideas of who we think we should be, and instead align with the way life *is*. It is comparable to a sharp exhalation when we realize the futility of the stress that made us tight. The idea of our own state of perfection is finally let go of in a loving embrace of our own idiosyncrasies. Without our own imperfections there could not be perfection, and this perfection that we already are is rarely perceived.

We put all of our energy into achieving the so-called goal of enlightenment because we are so dissatisfied with our own life as it is. We want everything to accord with our egotistical desires, enlightenment included. This is why we pine for enlightenment to be an event like something depicted by Hollywood. We are completely distracted from the perfection of our own life as it *is*. Enlightenment becomes just another victim of the fast-food culture built around us.

5
Fast-Food Spiritual Junkie

TO BELIEVE THAT ENLIGHTENMENT is just an event is to assume that you yourself are an event. But we know deep down this is not true, because we experience the beauty of life in its unified diversity. Our habits and tendencies—indoctrinated into us by culture, religion, and society—veil this beauty so that we view life itself as a mere event made up of numerous smaller events that entertain us while we pass through this life from birth to death.

Enlightenment thus becomes like any of the smaller events that we seek to experience in our life. We compartmentalize everything in order to have control over our life. We even attempt to control when and how we will become enlightened, as we bounce from one spiritual retreat to another, from one guru to another—and all the time this "enlightenment" is supposed to be right around the corner. But chasing enlightenment like this is really chasing just another pleasurable experience, the only difference being that this one is deemed as more spiritually aesthetic. We replace our old interests with spiritual interests, but this only does more damage because it masks the latent pain within our psyche. Born-again Christians and New Agers tend to mask their spiritual pain even more than others, because both groups believe they have spiritual knowledge over and above the ignorant masses. They view themselves as saved according to their doctrine, when in truth salvation comes only from within, from working through one's own pain.

Salvation does not come from an intellectual description within a doctrine; that would be irrational. Yet these irrational points of view are commonplace in our society, culture, and religions because we greedily want everything now, with the important word being *everything*. Salvation and enlightenment become commodified experiences that are treated like everything else in our world, as we eat them up and move on to the next experience.

Enlightenment thus is treated as a temporary phenomenon in our world. We believe that once we experience that moment we can move on to the next joyride. All of our experiences, enlightenment included, become compartmentalized into separate events that pass by for our convenience. We are like small children who crave more and more toys, yet get bored with them ever so quickly. Our fast-food culture consumes everything in its wake, leaving the earth behind as a mere rubbish dump. And this spills out into the rest of our life: from the way we eat, to the natural energy we consume, to the vain entertainment we seek, we become junkies to the drug of greed. We believe we have no problem, in the same way that addicts believe they have no problem, that they "can quit anytime."

Increasingly since the Industrial Revolution we have become the fast-food junkie generation who consume everything, leaving nothing behind. Momentary satisfaction is the stimulant of our greed. Yet we do not realize that anything of merely momentary value is valueless, particularly if we always have our eye on the future. We never truly enjoy any moment because we are seeking to be sedated by that moment.

Drugged by momentary satisfaction, we remain in a state of sleep, or hypnosis. Our fast-food junkie culture is a dreamlike state in which people act but are not conscious of what they do. The continual search for entertainment lulls us into the dream of future experience. Armenian mystic George Ivanovich Gurdjieff elaborates on this cultural hypnotic sleep in *In Search of the Miraculous*:

So long as a man sleeps profoundly and is wholly immersed in dreams he cannot even think about the fact that he is asleep. If he were to think that he was asleep, he would wake up. So everything goes on. And men have not the slightest idea what they are losing because of this sleep. As I have already said, as he is organized, that is, being such as nature has created him, man can be a self-conscious being. Such he is created and such he is born. But he is born among sleeping people, and, of course, he falls asleep among them just at the very time when he should have begun to be conscious of himself. Everything has a hand in this: the involuntary imitation of older people on the part of the child, voluntary and involuntary suggestion, and what is called "education." Every attempt to awaken on the child's part is instantly stopped. This is inevitable. And a great many efforts and a great deal of help are necessary in order to awaken later when thousands of sleep-compelling habits have been accumulated. And this very seldom happens. In most cases, a man when still a child already loses the possibility of awakening; he lives in sleep all his life and he dies in sleep. Furthermore, many people die long before their physical death.[1]

Greed becomes a part of life when we fixate on the future. We are not present to fully experience the moment that we seek pleasure from, because we are already busy planning the next experience. The mind is so busy in the compartmentalization of reality that it lacks the stillness to embrace the moment fully. A culture always striving for future success misses the point of life, as the point of life is in the immediate moment. Right here and now is where the real satisfaction of life is, and not in future moments to consume and discard. We become totally focused on temporary destinations with total disregard for the journey. Amazingly, we only appreciate the process of the journey when our time is up and we are on our deathbed.

But the growing awareness that eternity can be nowhere else but now becomes bastardized by our fast-food culture, put into spiritual boxes for intellectual convenience. People speak the flowery language of spirituality without truly understanding. In the first chapter of the

Tao Te Ching, Lao-tzu explains our propensity to try and intellectualize the mystery:

> *The tao that can be told*
> *is not the eternal Tao.*
> *The name that can be named*
> *is not the eternal Name.*
>
> *The unnamable is the eternally real.*
> *Naming is the origin*
> *of all particular things.*
>
> *Free from desire, you realise the mystery.*
> *Caught in desire, you see only the manifestations.*
>
> *Yet mystery and manifestations*
> *arise from the same source.*
> *This source is called darkness.*
>
> *Darkness within darkness.*
> *The gateway to all understanding.*[2]

Our fast-food culture is primarily intellectual, so anything claiming to be spiritual is really more up in the head than anything to do with the feeling realm of the heart, or, as Lao-tzu puts it, "darkness within darkness." Almost all religions are victims of this hypnosis. States of consciousness, such as enlightenment, fall prey to the clutches of such narrow hypnotic thinking. We misinterpret the eternal now and its resonance of enlightenment with our fast-food cultural terminology. We school ourselves on trying to understand this intellectually, but we lack the real intuitive feeling of that sense of unity.

In particular, many Westerners and also Easterners misrepresent and misunderstand the nondual schools of spirituality, parroting the words of masters such as Sri Ramana Maharshi without actually understanding them. One who has dived deep within understands that our perception of reality continues in its refinement through years of introspection. Even the words of a sage such as Sri Ramana Maharshi can mean something completely different now compared to what they seemed to say a year ago. This is the nature of the spiritual absolute within the relative world, because spiritual wisdom cannot be pinned down to a concrete interpretation. It is eternal and moves in correspondence to consciousness moving and merging with the irreducible essence of the universe.

Many students of nondual spirituality, especially Advaita Vedanta, have no awareness of this evolution because they confuse words, which are relative, with the actual experience, which is absolute. People interested in nondual teachings lack the ability, in most cases, to talk about spiritual topics without playing a subtle game of spiritual one-upmanship. They lack the psychological recognition of the feeling world of spirituality because their basic cognition is depleted from an intoxication of spiritual bypassing. The greed of the fast-food culture thus perverts even nondual philosophy into just another spiritual commodity.

The "get it now" mentality leads us to believe, in a purely intellectual way, that we are enlightened beings dwelling in nondual awareness. Arrogantly ignoring the psychological work to be done turns the esoteric student into a "fast-food spiritual junkie." As a result, many Westerners and also Easterners who claim to follow the nondual spiritual path often get drawn into a concrete universal interpretation, which is only intellectual, that is supposedly disconnected from the relative world.

Some sects within other paths, such as Taoism and Zen, can avoid this problem by incorporating into their training the psychological work needed to attain a true depth of being. Canadian spiritual psychotherapist Robert Augustus Masters explains this propensity our fast-food culture has to misinterpret teachings, especially those of nondualism:

It is very easy to intellectually appropriate nondual teachings and then use them to justify or rationalize some of our actions, such as disrespecting our or others' boundaries. . . . Truly recognizing the nondual nature of Reality leaves us not immune to the necessities of the everyday dualistic world but even more sensitive and attuned to them, even more capable of sanely and skillfully responding to them, and even more intimate with all that arises. . . .

Claims of abiding in nondual awareness run rampant in modern spiritual circles—and how could they not, given that we are deeply embedded in a culture slavishly devoted to quick fixes and highs, spiritual or otherwise? . . .

Hearing teachings that tell us we already are fully realized, nondual beings who have simply forgotten our true nature may reassure or console us, but in most cases it tends to distract from the work we truly need to do, which includes facing and working with our fear, aggression, greed, shame, and whatever else we've misused or turned away from in ourselves. The central shadow of pseudo-nondualistic teachings is unacknowledged dualism, which is most commonly characterized by a resolute aversion to acknowledging our need to do any in-depth psychological work.

An almost-universally acknowledged sage of the nondual, Ramana Maharshi spoke and acted from a nondual perspective simply because he could not do otherwise. Just as importantly, he wasn't looking for immunity from the raw stuff of life, and he sure wasn't busy being clever with language or theory. He was, in fact, radically available. . . .

While nondual teachings point out the futility of searching for what was never really lost, these teachings often fail to stress that such a search usually is not experienced as futile until it has been undertaken. Thus many spiritual seekers who believe in such teachings get stranded in a no-man's-land, supposedly "above" the developmental levels that they think they have transcended (but in fact have only intellectually skipped). This is what the great Buddhist teacher Nagarjuna meant when he mentioned the trap of *believing* in emptiness.[3]

The "get everything fast" mentality is unconsciously projected onto enlightenment as teachers and practitioners of spiritual practices and wisdom, especially nondualism, intellectually claim they are dwelling in the eternal abode of the universe in its innate "nowness." Those who believe this are still victims of the monarchical view of reality because they arrogantly believe they have figured out the game of life. To put life into a nice little spiritual package is to misunderstand that the universe is itself a mystery, and that each of us is an aspect of that mystery.

A fast-food spiritual junkie, like our culture in general, wants definitive answers about everything, including the mystery of life and our existence. We lack the foresight to see that our questions and even our answers are contrived. For example, there was once a Zen master in Japan who told his student that the next day he would like to see the student give a demonstration of Zen privately in the master's hermitage. Thrust into concern for pleasing the master, the student became anxious at the thought of such a demonstration of Zen. Being anxious all day and night, the student had no idea how to tackle this situation. Nervously going on his way to the master he spotted a peculiar wrinkled frog native to Japan and so he picked it up in the hope that this frog would exhibit Zen to his master. When the student presented the frog to the master, the master just shook his head and said this demonstration was too intellectual, meaning that it was too contrived and had required too much thought.

As we read in this story, there is no one right answer here, as Zen is to be completely engrossed in the spontaneity of the eternal now. But it is folly to think too much and attempt to plan our life. The master was trying to show, however esoterically, that there is no one right answer to his question or way to demonstrate Zen other than completely living it. There is no way to categorically explain the nondual awareness of the present moment because there is in a sense nothing to talk about.

The best example of this is when a monk asked the ninth-century Chinese Zen teacher Tung-shan Shou-ch'u "What is the Buddha?" to which Tung-shan answered, "Three pounds of flax." This answer is not so much *about* Zen but instead is *full of* Zen, as it takes the monk out of intellectual conceptualization. Zen Master Yuan-wu describes the depth of this irrational answer more beautifully:

> Various answers have been given by different masters to the question, "What is the Buddha?" . . . None, however, can excel T'ung-shan's "three pounds (*chin*) of flax" as regards its irrationality which cuts off all passage of speculation. Some comment that T'ung-shan was weighing flax at the moment, hence the answer. . . . Still others think that as the questioner was not conscious of the fact that he himself was the Buddha, T'ung-shan answered him in this indirect way. Such are all like corpses, for they are utterly unable to comprehend the living truth. There are still others who take "three pounds of flax" as the Buddha. What wild and fantastic remarks they make![4]

An in-depth knowledge that we are intrinsically and absolutely the Buddha cannot come immediately through intellectual understanding, even though it may help to clear out a lot of our conditioning, which blocks our energy from blending with universal energy.

When many people proclaim they live in nondual awareness in the present moment, they are only pretending and are actually lying to themselves. There does need to be a center of focus and sincerity in the great work of eternity, which requires us to look into those uncomfortable sides of ourselves and, instead of ignoring them by believing in our own intellectual spiritual profundity, begin to embrace our totality and work through the conditioned habits, tendencies, and pain that cripple our real and authentic enlightenment. This may appear to contradict what has been said thus far in regard to enlightenment within time, but it is not a contradiction. Due to the fact that our conditioning is the result of time, that means it needs a tender, stable, conscious attention in the present moment to begin to address and move through such time-bound obstacles.

But more often than not, that can't happen, because the sincerity of the spiritual seeker is lost in the intellectual game of spiritual one-upmanship. We need to keep in mind that this game is subtle, especially with people following nondual teachings, because most of the teachings consist of verbal discourse about pure awareness, rather than focusing on the world of intuitive perception and feeling, which are aspects of the spiritual world. There's nothing wrong with verbal discourse, as it is also essential, but we need to be mindful that it only points to pure awareness and is no substitute for actual experience.

The intuitive realm is seldom realized by the spiritually inclined, so many people stick to the intellectual sphere of doctrine and dogma, as this builds a false net of security for the individual to cling to, and in doing so escape doing any real self-work. This spiritual falsehood is the reason why certain groups of seekers, past and present, who had developed a heightened sense of intuition, decided to move away from those who are lost in doctrine and dogma.

Jesus of Nazareth once mentioned, "Don't cast your pearls before swine." This means do not give wisdom to those who are not ready to hear it. From this perspective we can see the reasoning behind creating secret societies, as the masses only understand truth intellectually. Secret societies can allow spiritual seekers to get away from violently ignorant dogmatists, even though one could argue that the secrecy lacks compassion for many potential seekers who remain victims of the monarchical view and fast-food culture.

Nowadays, though, we have a better chance of finding more intimate dialogue about such spiritual matters. The individual self-work we all need to embrace can facilitate a greater collective dialogue. If we don't push our boundaries and jump out of our comfortable boxes into what sociologist and researcher Kingsley L. Dennis calls having "no box," then we will make no progress, let alone realize that enlightenment is innately ours now. Our tendency as fast-food spiritual junkies is to ignore and run far away from sincere self-work, because it is easier to turn spiritual seeking into just another source of entertainment. We can see this tendency with the various forms of New Age "entertainment," namely mediums, and particularly channeling, psychics, and connecting with angels and other "higher beings." Though some of these mediums may be genuine and well grounded, their methods invariably fall into misuse at the hands of those who use them to make money and entertain. We become distracted when spirituality turns into a means for entertainment and dogma.

ENTERTAINMENT IS DISTRACTION

Entertainment in itself can inspire, or it can keep people asleep. The main reason why entertainment is such a big part of our culture is for the latter: keeping humanity asleep. The art expressed through entertainment is secondary, and not truly appreciated because the masses are hypnotized. The majority of people never truly take in deeply the art of another, as their greed distracts them from the present moment.

Real art is not appreciated in our culture, which is reflected in the way that budget cuts in schooling usually begin with art and leave courses such as economic studies untouched. This depreciation of art leads us into more artificial and tacky media such as reality television, which reflect our fast-food culture, as they are produced and disappear faster than we can say "abracadabra!" Real inspiration through art is secondary to money and the market industry. We are distracted from what really matters in life, and in this case we value money more than artful inspiration.

Our modern culture, in general, is under this spell, as many people waste their life in jobs they don't even like and so are wasting their time making money to go on wasting time to make more money. The money we make allows us to pay for more entertainment, which only distracts us from the present moment and our innate being. Our society is built on distraction because the individual is distracted by the incessant movements of mind. In *The Wisdom of Insecurity,* Alan Watts explores this perpetual anxiety within the mind of our world:

When belief in the eternal becomes impossible, and there is only the poor substitute of belief in believing, men seek their happiness in the joys of time. However much they may try to bury it in the depths of their minds, they are well aware that these joys are both uncertain and brief. This has two results. On the one hand, there is the anxiety that one may be missing something, so that the mind flits nervously and greedily from one pleasure to another, without finding rest and satisfaction in any. On the other, the frustration of having always to pursue a future good in a tomorrow which never comes, and in a world where everything must disintegrate, gives men an attitude of "What's the use anyhow?"

Consequently our age is one of frustration, anxiety, agitation, and addiction to "dope." Somehow we must grab what we can while we can, and drown out the realization that the whole thing is futile and meaningless. This "dope" we call our high standard of living, a violent and complex stimulation of the senses, which makes them progressively less sensitive and thus in need of yet more violent stimulation. We crave distraction—a panorama of sights, sounds, thrills, and titillations into which as much as possible must be crowded in the shortest possible time.

To keep up this "standard" most of us are willing to put up with lives that consist largely in doing jobs that are a bore, earning the means to seek relief from the tedium by intervals of hectic and expensive pleasure. These intervals are supposed to be the real living, the real purpose served by the necessary evil of work. . . .

This is no caricature. It is the simple reality of millions of lives, so commonplace that we need hardly dwell upon the details, save to note the anxiety and frustration of those who put up with it, not knowing what else to do.[5]

The self-work an individual has to undertake is on all planes of consciousness—physical, mental, and spiritual—because if we ignore the totality of our being then we ignore aspects of ourselves that need to become conscious. When we are not engaged in self-work we become easily distracted because we have no center of gravity. Distraction is the result of our lack of understanding in regard to our original consciousness. We seek vain entertainment as a result to keep us distracted from reality as it truly *is*.

Distraction via entertainment invariably leads us into artificiality and imitation, as we have no understanding of who we truly are. We paint an image of ourselves in our mind based on others, who are invariably within the sphere of entertainment. Women pile chemicals on their faces, and men overdo it at the gym, hoping someday they can look like those celebrities, whose appearance is often the result of plastic surgery and computerized photo retouching. We incorrectly assume that we are not naturally beautiful, so we seek to somehow enhance ourselves by imitating others in the hope that we will be accepted by a society and culture who created this whole foolish game in the first place. We are distracted in this case by trying to be somebody that we aren't. Many people's lives are dedicated to this complete attainment of imitation, ignoring the fact that we are already perfect just the way we are.

The belief of our fast-food culture is that the way nature intended life to be is somehow a mistake and requires our artificial intervention. Our interference with the individual's natural process of life, both physical and mental, confuses us even more as we begin to chase an artificial self built based on what we see in our entertainment. American actor Brad Pitt's character Tyler Durden in the film *Fight Club* explains beautifully the frustration people find themselves in when they are chasing the distraction of money, fame, and materialism:

Man, I see in Fight Club the strongest and smartest men who've ever lived. I see all this potential, and I see it squandered. God damn it, an entire generation pumping gas, waiting tables—slaves with white collars. Advertising has us chasing cars and clothes, working jobs we hate so we can buy shit we don't need. We're the middle children of history, man. No purpose or place. We have no Great War. No Great Depression. Our great war is a spiritual war. Our great depression is our lives. We've all been raised on television to believe that one day we'd all be millionaires, and movie gods, and rock stars, but we won't. And we're slowly learning that fact. And we're very, very pissed off.[6]

Being completely engrossed in the distraction of entertainment keeps us in a deep sleep, with our eyes open even though nobody is home. To chase another's dreams is to discard your own uniqueness and divinity. In Taoist wisdom this uniqueness is known as *li* (理) in Chinese, which we mentioned earlier. It refers to an individual's organic pattern within consciousness, in other words, divine uniqueness.

We also commit this crime against ourselves on our journey into enlightenment when people begin to imitate their teachers, or parrot scripture word for word. In this regard spirituality can also distract you from your own true nature. Disciples of a guru can lose their way by passively following and agreeing with everything the guru says. The guru ends up becoming just another form of entertainment for the disciples. People waste hours upon hours only listening to the guru's words without assimilating what is being said. Day after day, year after year, people listen to their guru without gaining more wisdom, simply as entertainment or music to their ears, which actually keeps them more asleep than ever.

The New Age gurus who promote only positivity and nondualism often acquire a lot of followers because there is no real self-work to be done that confronts an individual's psychology head-on. These teachers who only push positivity are purely a source of entertainment, keeping their followers hypnotized. The fundamental truth that enlightenment is *right now* is convoluted by New Age spiritual gurus who have no real depth of wisdom. As a result, this wisdom becomes subject to a misinterpretation of oneness, with big-picture discussions with no relation to the relative, and with a basic misunderstanding of spirituality and enlightenment.

In the modern era, as a result of misunderstanding, spirituality has become more about marketing than enlightenment. And we can be assured that anything to do with marketing is more about money and entertainment than the healing and enlightenment of the individual and world. A common trait of the followers of these New Age gurus is they acquire the artificial and absurd notion that they have already arrived at enlightenment because they intellectually believe so, and also because the guru intellectually said so. The real sense of unity is not discussed because in most cases the followers and the gurus are disconnected from the natural energetic feeling and spontaneous world of consciousness. New Age positivity spirituality is developing a way of understanding that is stuck in the head, rather than a sincere humility felt deeply within the heart.

A spirituality only in the head has no real depth of understanding that our innate enlightenment is what we already are, because if it is only in the head then it is lost in intellectual speculation. Distracted by such speculation, we cease to really feel the oneness that the New Age positivity pushers perpetuate because the real sense of unity has nothing to do with anything that can be artificially created or induced. In reality it is a process of nature and also belongs to nature.

6
Enlightenment Is Natural, Not Artificially Induced

THE REAL SENSE OF UNITY at the core of enlightenment is eclipsed by the overstimulation of our relative existence. People take up a spiritual practice for a lifetime and somehow never attain enlightenment. This happens because the art of the practice is thought to induce such a state as enlightenment, while our relative being—our ego—goes on through life with its habits, tendencies, and idiosyncrasies unchecked. Many people practice yoga, t'ai chi, meditation, and so on, but continue to live imbalanced through their need to overstimulate the senses. Now, I'm not saying here that we should discard all sensory experiences, as that is impossible. But bad habits and tendencies become "bad" when there is a propensity for excess.

If we are more conscious of our being, we have an intuitive feeling when a particular part of our life is out of balance. When a part of our being is out of balance it is because we have overcompensated for that aspect with excess. This is best reflected in our diets, as our epidemic food issues, from obesity to anorexia, are the result of imbalance in those peoples' lives. Obesity, for example, is usually the result of psychological imbalance, as we tend to mask the pain with unhealthy tasty foods. An individual suffering from obesity as a result of unhealthy habits finds it difficult to have the realization of enlightenment, because the greed of excessive food intake veils that intuitive faculty of our innate connection with the universe. This is not to say that anybody who is obese cannot realize enlightenment—there are of course many cases of obese people attaining enlightenment—but in general one's whole being is out of balance within the physical and mental planes of consciousness.

At the opposite extreme are those who are too rigid and strict in their diet. Some vegans and vegetarians would surely fit into this category. There is nothing wrong with being conscious about your diet, but when you are overly concerned about everything you eat, then subtle forms of stress develop within your body and mind. Both extremes lack balance.

When one realizes one's own imbalances, one becomes more attracted to spiritual practices because they are thought of as a medicine for our relative ills. This is true in one sense and false on the other. It is true because spiritual practices will center your focus if they are backed up by dedicated discipline; but it is false because the excessive imbalance that made our ills begins to be projected into our spiritual practice. Once our spiritual practice becomes excessive it loses its natural flexibility and enters the intellectual domain of becoming rigid to attain the "goal" of enlightenment. We then become imbalanced in our spiritual practice because it has more to do with repetition and anxiety than anything to do with liberation.

Almost all spiritual paths are vexed by this paradox, as the majority of traditions stick to excessive discipline. But as Gautama the Buddha realized after his six years as an ascetic, no matter how hard he strived for enlightenment it continually alluded him. It was only when he completely let go of all his searching and accepted a milky soup from a young farm girl under the shade of the Bodhi tree that he realized he was searching and striving for what is intrinsic to our nature: enlightenment. Paradoxically though, the Buddha needed to be on his journey in the first place in order to realize this. We could say that it was absurd for him to undergo six rigorous years of asceticism to realize what is ever-present right now, but we lose sight of the fact that without those six years he could not have become enlightened.

If Gautama the Buddha were not at first deluded by intellectual striving, and at the same time sincere on his search, then there would have been nothing for him to let go of in this life. There would have been no attachment to eclipse his spiritual perception. It is only when we realize how we are attached to those aspects of our self that hide our connection with the universe that we can know the freedom of being detached. This is a paradox, but the mystery of life exists in paradox. The Buddha's Middle Way arises from this mysterious paradox, and this paradox is essentially why only a rare few truly discover the Middle Way, because it is beyond the sphere of category and discernment.

This paradox is not usually contemplated in New Age spirituality, because first of all its depth is too great for many people to comprehend; and second, because it implies that there is still an immense amount of self-work to do on the relative side of our being. An artificial spirituality comes into existence when we just take the pleasurable aspects of any story and build our foundation upon that.

In the case of New Age spirituality, the complete letting-go aspect of Gautama the Buddha's story is highlighted, while the rest of it is ignored. People are taught to forget about spiritual practice or any desire they have, especially for enlightenment, because all you have to do is let go, and enlightenment will be your reality. Though this sounds like a sweet deal, for those of us who are authentic and sincere with ourselves we know that, without being supported by spiritual growth in the relative world, then this letting-go is only a half-truth. New Age pop-spirituality overlooks the fact that the absolute realm of mystery is in direct relationship to the relative world. Or, to paraphrase the Heart Sutra, form implies formlessness and formlessness implies form, in the same way that the universe produces consciousness and consciousness evokes the universe.

Yet this wisdom is completely misinterpreted by the majority of spiritual teachers, who incorrectly assume and teach their disciples that the world of form must be transcended rather than embraced and loved completely. This rejection of the world of form is also in line with the Christian doctrine that heaven is some place "good" people go after death, which is in contrast to the reality that heaven is right here and now where eternity actually *is*. We always discover in such vain attempts to transcend the relative world that no matter how wise we think we are or skilled at spiritual practice, we will continue to come crashing down against the limitations of life from trying to stand above it. This sort of attitude toward the relative aspect of the universe is almost like we are trying to get "the upper hand" on the universe.

The concept of transcendence is usually thought of in the same sense, but this is an abstraction of its real spiritual significance. The real spiritual significance of transcendence means going beyond the idea of who you think you are. The idea of who we think we are has strength only when we believe the relative side of our being is the totality of our existence. Many people have no intuitive sense of that absolute eternal aspect of themselves, so we fall for the limitations of time that distract us from that irreducible essence.

Real transcendence implies self-work and stepping through the artificial aspects of our being. In the face of real self-work, we realize that we overestimate ourselves with our modern pop-spiritualty. We develop an arrogant attitude toward self-work as we attempt to eat only the cream of the Buddha's story without acknowledging the whole cake. Again, enlightenment as the resonance of the eternal now is misunderstood by those who lack the real sense of unity felt from that state. We believe that we can let go of everything and just try to remain present while we bypass all that makes us suffer, which is an egotistical reaction to enlightenment stemming from the monarchical view of the universe.

We have a fast-food approach to enlightenment, which slowly develops an artificial characteristic of mind in an individual who only intellectually believes they are enlightened. A lot of people wax lyrical about being "nothing," or "empty," or that they live in "oneness." But if you test them by either questioning their intellectual statements or by simply stomping on their feet you will become aware of their suppressed anger and repressed pain when they snap at you like vicious wolves. The oneness and being nothing or empty that many people speak of is really just their pretending to be enlightened with no real sense of unity in reality. This "enlightenment" is artificial and is cloaked by vanity on the individual's part. Astonishingly in this example, we are not really even trying to induce enlightenment, but instead, we are just pretending, in the same way that politicians pretend to be good citizens.

In this sense we treat enlightenment as a mere intellectual accessory to show off to other people. With such people, spiritual practices become more of a circus act than anything naturally sincere. We strive to be the best at performing yoga asanas and to sound the wisest in discourse, and all of it misses the point.

This can only happen if we delude ourselves into believing that we have transcended the world and now see the world as God does. We cannot just have a phase transition of consciousness simply because we intellectually decide to. There has to be real fundamental change within your being, which occurs on all three planes of consciousness— physical, mental, and spiritual. To ignore any aspect of yourself is to treat your being with neglect. Usually the aspects of ourselves that we ignore become the artificial parts of ourselves that we assume are natural.

In our culture and society it becomes normal for individuals not to be conscious of their own latent habits and tendencies. As a result we dive headfirst into an excessiveness that keeps us distracted from reality. Reality can only be experienced when we make a conscious effort to eradicate the excessiveness in our lives that distracts us from our original nature. These distractions in our life can be so subtle that we find ourselves defending these temporary illusions, as we incorrectly identify them as our original nature.

These are symptoms of our fast-food, get-it-now culture, which is built around sense activity and the overstimulation of the senses. As a result, many people turn to what stimulates their senses for emotional comfort, whether to experience joy or to mask our pain. We want everything in life to be easy, because then our pain is not brought out into the open and exposed. Our modern misconceptions of spiritual wisdom, especially in the New Age, reflect this easy come, easy go attitude. In focusing only on the glamorous side of the Buddha's journey, we believe that our enlightenment should be in line with our fast-food appetite.

Our fast-food culture is built on the notion that everything should be free and easy, so we go ahead and take what we believe is ours. Like spoiled children, we become bored with what stimulates our senses and we want more than we can handle. Enlightenment is based on this "free" ideology of our fast-food culture, which is a way of discarding the journey. In our greed we want everything quick and easy as a result of our social angst. Yet the essence of enlightenment is not comparable to social angst or fast-food ideologies. As Gautama the Buddha realized, freedom is not free, but it is our original nature.

FREEDOM IS NOT FOR FREE BUT IT IS OUR NATURE

Freedom is not for free but it is our original nature, which is curiously paradoxical. Let's not confuse this original natural freedom with the freedom of our fast-food culture. This debt owed to spiritual freedom means the honesty, sincerity, and authenticity of an individual's search for enlightenment is an ultimate desire that the universe does reciprocate. Those who tend to be lazy in any facet of life, especially in a sincere approach to enlightenment, usually never have any deep understanding other than an intellectual one. This is why many people who have an interest in spiritual wisdom usually just like to talk about it rather than engage in self-work and sincere introspection. Laziness in this regard is erroneously associated with the Taoist principle of wu-wei (無為, nondoing and nonforcing). So many spiritually inclined people misinterpret such wisdom to justify their own laziness.

The effortlessness of wu-wei becomes the fruit of an individual's life when their world comes into order with the natural order of the universe, known as Tao in Chinese or Brahman in Sanskrit. Wu-wei is an experience lived by the individual that brings a divine grace into their life, as it is the harmonious function of reality and in truth the way things are. Wu-wei has nothing to do with laziness, as you can be effortlessly in motion. The principle of wu-wei is the way all aspects of nature *are,* while laziness is a function of the ego.

Laziness is wound up in the makeup of the ego because it is always about postponement into an unknowable future. The ego constantly puts things off, especially of the creative nature, because it never wants to face reality as it is right now. Freedom from the limitations of the ego requires us to live completely present and engaged in all the methods that make the ego cringe and seek postponement, such as spiritual practice and exercising the creative mind, namely through art. When we begin sincere spiritual practice and a love for creative expression, we discover that these modalities of consciousness are somehow in relation to the higher self, which we usually only read about in books. The creative mind is the spiritual mind, and this may answer some questions as to why our world is the way it is, because it stems from a gross lack of creativity.

Spiritual practice and creativity go hand in hand because the discipline and focus in spiritual practice allows for a heightened state of concentration and closer contact with intuition in creative work. It is true that when we are in such a whole state of being through practice and creativity we begin to cultivate a deeper relationship with universal essence (known as Tao, Brahman, God, and so on). In Hinduism this relationship is known as the connection between Atman (universal essence manifesting as the Self/undifferentiated consciousness) and Brahman. This connection, or we should say original home, is that deep part of our mind where the sense of unity is lived and perceived. The ego eclipses this awareness because its functioning is diametrically opposed to nature, as it is a linear construct that is obviously out of accord with the nonlinearity of nature. The ego distinguishes itself as separate from the universe and thus lives in a tiny isolated place of understanding, which leads to laziness as it lives with the fear of being separate from the whole universe.

The laziness of the ego cons us into the belief that our enlightenment is free and so there is no need to engage with external reality. Our freedom and enlightenment are not actually free or enlightened, considering we guard ourselves in a overprotective spiritual bubble, which is really only a cult of one. Real enlightenment is to understand that self and other go together, as do Atman and Brahman, because they are intrinsically the same.

Our original enlightened nature is free because it can never be other than you. But over time this original nature becomes covered over with the accumulation of experience that builds the solidified, separate ego. We shouldn't ignore experience, but instead we should understand it not from the position of opposition, which is what our society and culture promote. Experience should be embraced, as it is part of our journey. The ego resists experience, especially when it is thought to be unpleasant and not in accord with our egotistical beliefs. If there is no introspection to perceive the constraints of this separate ego, then the awareness of our original enlightened nature will become convoluted and basically false. This is not to say that the relative and absolute worlds are separate; they do go together as self and other do. But the problem arises when the individual identifies only with the relative, personal world of the ego.

This is what is meant by "freedom is not free," because you do owe a debt and the payment is deposited in the refinement of your separate ego. The refinement is based on your own sincere self-work. But keep in mind that as long as you have a human body and mind you will always have an ego, but so long as the ego sees itself as separate from everything else, it will reject any perception that contradicts that separateness. This is why to perceive the infinite in all things requires sincere self-work.

HOW NON-DOING CAN LEAD TO
SPIRITUAL PRIDE AND EMOTIONAL NUMBNESS

The modern belief in spiritual nondual teachings is that we have literally nothing to do to realize the undifferentiated consciousness of the Self, that is, Atman. Under the spiritual umbrella of a nondual teacher we are taught to just continually observe the chattering ego within us, with a complete disregard for everything else in the universe.

This is a very centered mode of practice, but it can become self-absorbed. For example, people who follow nondual teachings often isolate themselves in their own introspection through believing that everything that is happening to them from the external world is an illusion and only something for them to get over. While this may be true in one sense, from a practical perspective it is disastrously false, because when people in this mode of practice take in abuse from other people, for example, they assume that their suffering from such abuse is really their problem, and not that of their abuser. This is absurd considering that many people naturally respond to the external world spontaneously with no forethought. But this is not to say that we should respond to the external world with emotional abandon, because if we truly look within, our response to environmental stimuli should be more consciously natural, from a pure mind. One of the key aspects of nondual teachings is a psychological tool and attitude called *vairagya* (वैराग्य) in Sanskrit. Vairagya means nonreaction, which can be mistakenly thought of by teachers and students as complete negation of reality itself. The practice of vairagya actually means that what we experience in the inner and outer world is not reacted to without time for assimilation and only then can we choose if action is required as each situation is different.

Some teachers and students of nonduality make the error of misunderstanding practices such as vairagya and believing the external world is an illusion, which leads to a repression of natural emotions that cause subtle psychological imbalances. An individual attracted to this understanding of nondual teachings becomes even more egocentric, as they begin to overanalyze and think too much about their observation and self-enquiry. We can become conscious of this egocentric approach to self-enquiry when we realize our reactions to life and response to the external world are only intellectual, contrived by our mistaken understanding of nondual concepts. We find ourselves thinking too much before any speech or action, which is as confused a state as we were in before we discovered such spiritual teachings. This subtle, intellectually contrived perspective pervades almost all spiritual paths through our attempts to try and induce the original enlightened nature. To induce anything in life is an impulse from the artificial tendencies of mind, ego for example. To induce is to imply that you are not part of nature, that you are not in fact natural. We cannot induce a state of consciousness that is innate within our being. We cannot fall into intellectual speculation dressed in spiritual robes.

The artificial realm of life infiltrates our spiritual practices and basic self-work, and many people attempt to intellectually induce behaviors and states of consciousness, revealing themselves as arrogantly lazy, believing they are at the mountaintop of understanding. Such lack of humility is the red flag of inauthenticity. The real challenge of sincere self-work is to uproot our artificiality and return to the natural order of the universe. This can only happen without trying to induce or to think about it. It has to be as natural as growing hair—no *doing* is needed.

The Taoist wisdom and terminology for this naturalness is the Chinese *tzu-jan* (自然), which means that which is spontaneously of itself. As a natural organism is in harmony with all life, it grows of itself spontaneously without external compulsion. Nature, tzu-jan, will grow spontaneously of itself when it is not restricted by external limitations and influences. Tzu-jan can only arise of itself without external compulsion. The principle of tzu-jan is the essence of the yoking process found within the spiritual core of most religions, and especially in the origins of Chinese and Indian wisdom. When we retract from our conditioned perception of reality, or involution in other terminology, we come back into nature and grow spontaneously in harmony with all other components of nature.

Enlightenment is not a state of consciousness we can induce, as Gautama the Buddha realized. But it is an aspect of our being that is in accord with the pure feeling realm of consciousness opposed to the intellectual sphere. The pure intuitive feeling of enlightenment is expressed through the fragrance of stillness within our mind. This is true self-enquiry and mindfulness, as without effort or forethought we come into the world as it naturally *is*. Nature is stillness, and so is enlightenment, completely present with no need to induce or speculate. Problems arise only when we step out of this original nature.

To be natural in a world based on artificiality is foreign. We are infected with numerous degrees of artificiality, which eclipse our resonance with the universe. The realization of enlightenment is hindered by our artificiality. All of our attempts are futile, yet paradoxically we should not give up. We need a level of attunement to the feeling of the heart rather than the discernment of the head. Somehow our spiritual practices and self-work have to become natural without our intention to do so.

7
Enlightened Attunement

EARLIER WE DISCUSSED the differences between superficial and occult initiation. The superficiality of knowledge and understanding is prevalent in our highly scientific and intellectual world, because to delve into anything purely experiential is far too occult for the majority of people, and so is often ignorantly labeled as mere "mystical speculation." The masses are bound by distraction, so they attempt to understand life and their very existence from this deluded state of mind. The subtle language of consciousness is far too vague for the profane, as symbology, sacred geometry, meditation, myth, spiritual principles, and so on are not open to scientific experimentation and categorical interpretation. But the scientific community loses sight of how their observation of what they call "facts" ultimately changes over time, as humanity achieves ever greater understanding. It is not possible to pin down nature with definitions and words. German physicist and Nobel laureate Werner Heisenberg states in *Physics and Philosophy*: "We have to remember that what we observe is not nature herself, but nature exposed to our method of questioning."[1]

Classical science would have us believe that the map is itself the territory. To experience nature as it is, science assumes that our calculations and words will spawn this experience. But isn't it absurd to confuse the map with the territory? When we travel into unknown lands it is smart to have a map to guide you, but never do we confuse the map with the actual experience of the territory. As the Polish-American philosopher and scientist Alfred Korzybski famously stated, "The map is not the territory."[2]

The problem in our world is that we confuse the map with the territory. Science does this in exploring the nature of matter, as if it can somehow explain the existence of the universe. Science and religion are exactly the same in this regard, as religion uses scripture to somehow explain God. Like science, religion confuses the map with the territory. Religion binds people to the belief that the "word of God" and the so-called "law of God" are bound to scripture. All sorts of dogmas and psychosis are spawned as a result.

Most religions of the world are only superficial, lacking any depth or healing for the individual. Wound up in the superficial sphere of scripture, one loses sight that religious scriptures were intended to intuitively reveal something deeper in us. They were not meant to be taken literally, as if the map itself was the territory. The literal interpretation is only superficial, and is the reason why those who misinterpret religious scriptures as literal usually have a subtle but violently dogmatic psychosis.

That mysterious world that we know nothing about exists within us in the deeper recesses of our psyche. It is usually through the occult paths of myth, symbology, and metaphor that we can gain a glimpse of that unknowable void. Understanding religious scripture and even the scientific explorations of nature as pure mythological archetypal symbols is thought of as a blasphemy by those who are hypnotized by literal interpretation of mystery. American mythologist Joseph Campbell explains some of the reasons why we have turned our back on the love for the mystical world:

> I think what happens in our mythology here in the West is that the mythological archetypal symbols have come to be interpreted as facts. Jesus *was* born of a virgin. Jesus *was* resurrected from the dead. Jesus *went* to heaven by ascension. Unfortunately, in our age of scientific skepticism we know these things did not actually hap-

pen, and so the mythic forms are called falsehoods. The word *myth* now means falsehood, and so we have lost the symbols and that mysterious world of which they speak. . . .

At present, our culture has rejected this world of symbology. It has gone into an economic and political phase, where spiritual principles are completely disregarded. You may have practical ethics and that kind of thing, but there is no spirituality in any aspect of our contemporary Western civilization. Our religious life is ethical, not mystical. The mystery has gone and society is disintegrating as a result. . . .

We take the Old Testament God to be fact, not a symbol. The Holy Land is a specific place and no other, man is superior to the beasts, and nature has fallen. With the Fall in the Garden of Eden, nature becomes a corrupt force, so we do not give ourselves to nature as Chief Seattle did. We will correct nature. We develop ideas of good and evil in nature, and we are supposed to be on the side of the good, which creates an obvious tension. We don't yield to nature. The term *nature religions* has become the object of rejection and abuse. But what else are you going to worship? Some figment of your imagination that you have put up in the clouds? A strange thing has happened. It is so extreme that if you don't believe in a figure, you don't have any worship. Now everything is lost![3]

Religions treat enlightenment as science treats matter, which is a result of this absurd impulse to identify only with the literal interpretation. With deeper occult initiations, as opposed to superficial initiations, we discover a greater level of understanding if we can peek into the esoteric heart of religious scripture, and even of matter itself. What accounts for this greater level of wisdom? This deeper wisdom doesn't make one a better person, but those with a greater wisdom have a better chance of stepping into the light of enlightenment. So what accounts for this greater level of understanding? To understand this we need to have a greater perspective on how people can attune themselves.

Those who are sincere in their own introspection and self-work begin to be aware of a higher state of consciousness almost foreign to the dualistic consciousness of the masses. This is not only perceptual, but also in how we understand ourselves in relation to the universe. In the occult initiation of purusha (pure awareness), this level of attunement is the fruit of such refined perception. From the ability to see ourselves and the universe as it *is*, a new level of attunement dawns on our consciousness without any desire to do so. This attunement is very much a natural aspect of our consciousness, in the same way that we grow hair. Few people become conscious of this attunement to reality, to this higher state of consciousness. As religion and science have grown further and further apart, with each side becoming increasingly dogmatic, they became more skeptical of experiential knowledge because the superficial aspect of the physical world took pride of place.

According to religion and science this attuned aspect of consciousness is the pure speculation of an occult practitioner, and according to both it is like trying to prove the existence of the Loch Ness Monster. In this regard both religion and science leave out the basic experiential realm of life and consciousness.

In ancient times, when religion and science were one and the same, at their heart was mysticism. Mysticism is solely concerned with the inner and outer worlds, yet both are deemed as one through a higher level of attunement, that is, *gnosis*, which comes from the Greek word meaning experiential knowledge of the divine mystery. The enlightened sage has such a higher level of attunement for wisdom and gnosis. Both religion and science want to eradicate the mystical perspective because it destroys the illusory ideology of the monarchical view of reality. Our consciousness remains in a state of infancy as a result. To attune our whole being to a clearer perception and greater understanding threatens the social, cultural, and religious establishment. A sage is attuned to a mystical reality beyond normal comprehension, where love, harmony, and unassociated joy are the everyday bread of life. What would it take for the individual to reach a purer level of attunement and escape the clutches of artificiality?

CRISES OF PERCEPTION AND UNDERSTANDING

Our view is too narrow and our understanding is too convoluted. Both result from the artificial views foisted upon the individual by social, cultural, and religious institutions, who have lost the fundamental meaning of life to a pedagogical approach to life. From birth we are constantly hypnotized so that we fall in line with what is socially acceptable in our world. We never question the motives of society, culture, and religion because all the so-called adults have fallen victim to this programmed hypnosis.

The majority of people in the world operate from this state of hypnosis. We identify with power external to us, so we begin to associate our being with group ideological structures, which manifest as nationalism, racism, sexism, and religions. Yet we lack the understanding that groupthink is an illusion because in reality these group ideological structures don't exist. The only reason people believe any group exists is because the individuals who make up the group agree that it exists. When we form an attitude built on group identification we begin to behave artificially because we have removed ourselves from our true state of authentic individuality. We as individuals are never the group; we have only been conditioned to think we are, and it is entirely our choice to sever this illusionary bond. Only then can we become sovereign over our own consciousness as nature intended it.

When we build a framework of understanding that gives our innate power over to soulless entities—meaning any group—then that state of hypnotic psychology infects all aspects of our life. Our relationships, diets, and general ways of living all become artificial. All of these aspects affect our whole being whether we like it or not. When we can perceive the totality of our life as an individual, we can become aware of the aspects in our life that affect all other parts. Generally people compartmentalize their life because our artificial perception does not believe that all parts go together as one. The crisis of this perception results from how we are lost in the details of worldly affairs and cannot see reality as it *is*. Our lack of real understanding affects our perception, as artificial mental habits and tendencies imply that our perception will be obscured as a result.

Society, organized religion, and culture intoxicate our minds so we believe only in a world of matter, while everything else is treated as purely mystical speculation. This general way of thinking has caused much harm to humanity and the planet because this ideology promotes isolated separateness to the whole. In perceiving reality only as finite, we have a kindergarten understanding of our place in the universe. It is a crisis of consciousness, but it is more correctly a crisis brought about by our lack of understanding and our polluted perception. Our understanding is that we are a stranger in these lands, so our perception of reality is based on a reality that rules us like a king or in most cases as an enemy. To understand that there are higher levels of attunement is not even an issue for those whose beings are polluted with artificiality. Most people trapped in this hypnosis are not even conscious of the fact that the ability to develop an individual personality distinct from your original nature—created from the outside in—implies that you are part of a much larger reality than the one you feel is encased only within your skin. To expand our horizons of knowledge about the self and the universe allows for the process of attunement to begin.

TRANSFORMING ENERGY IS THE CURRENCY OF ATTUNEMENT

To expand our consciousness we need to realize that our perception of separateness and the false understanding of a finite solid reality is drastically outdated. From the standpoint of mysticism, ancient esoteric metaphysics, and new fields of science, energy has to be included in our common way of thinking about the world and ourselves.

In our outdated mode of perception and understanding we exclude energy. We exclude the planet's electromagnetic field of energy, energy from the motions and movements of planetary bodies, and not to mention the condensed energy of matter. If we do include this universal perspective of energy into the ordinary fabric of thinking, we get a deeper insight into the nature of reality.

We discover that everything is energy, including your entire being. From this awareness, everything we experience in life is actually a transaction of energy and also a transformation of energy. The fundamental ways we transform energy are through the food we eat, liquid we drink, air we breathe, and the impressions we take in through our eyes and ears. The way we transact energy with other people depends on how we transform energy. Transforming energy equates to what we take in through our senses. Everything we transform through our senses contributes to the energy we emanate in the world. In the same way that we view the energy of natural resources as fuel, what we take in through our senses is the fuel that determines our level of attunement to our original beingness.

SENSORY ATTUNEMENT

In the Hindu philosophy of Vedanta, humans are thought to have six senses. The original five senses of sight, hearing, taste, smell, and touch determine the function of the sixth sense, thoughts. Thoughts are influenced from what we consume through the other five senses, as these five senses will transform your thoughts which will determine your level of attunement. This knowledge is not isolated to Vedanta but it is also found in other wisdom traditions and their symbology. The Egyptian symbol of the Eye of Horus, personified in the Egyptian goddess Wadjet, is one such symbol. Superficially, the Eye of Horus is thought of as a symbol referring to protection, royal power, and good health. But esoterically it conceals the ancient philosophy of the six senses.

1/8 = Thought

1/4 = Sight

1/2 = Smell

1/16 = Hearing

1/32 = Taste

1/64 = Touch

Figure 7.1. The Eye of Horus Six-Sense Philosophy
Illustration by Daniel A. Stewart

In the symbolism of the Eye of Horus the component parts of the symbol make up the six senses of the human being, as you can see in figure 7.1. The eye in this symbol is significant because when we transform energy more purely our attunement to reality becomes refined and as a result our perception evolves out of the detail of life. This is symbolized by the eye itself. This attunement and evolved perception becomes natural to consciousness when we gain awareness that what we take in through the nine gates of the human being transforms our entire energetic structure. The nine gates in esoteric wisdom are the two eyes, two ears, two nostrils, mouth, anus, and penis or vagina. The fuel (that is, sensations) we take in through the nine gates stimulate the six senses and determines our level of attunement to reality, both inner and outer. Like anything in this world, the purer the fuel the higher the level of energy transformation.

Enlightenment right now becomes eclipsed when we take in fuel dominated by artificial stimulants. Many people eat processed food that only hypersensitizes the taste buds and sedates our sense of smell; they watch and listen to news and vain entertainment that make us believe that those illusionary dramas are real; and they have an over-stimulated sex life more like that of animals than anything human. These examples are only a few compared to the magnitude of our sense activity.

We oversensitize ourselves in the hope that this momentary pleasure will alleviate our latent pain. The term *moderation* has no meaning in a world bound to the excessiveness of seeking pleasure. Pleasure in this world is what sedates us, what keeps us in a state of hypnotic sleep with our eyes open but with nobody home. We overstimulate our sight, hearing, taste, smell, and touch with unnatural activity and imbalanced pleasures, which disturb the natural function of the sixth sense of thinking. Thought vibrations become out of sync with our natural being, which leads us into all sorts of suffering. All of this has been caused by our attraction to an unnatural way of living, because our society and culture promotes such artificiality as the pinnacle of life.

Yet the more we overstimulate our senses the more we are disconnected from the source of our own being. As a result we exhibit an artificial life that is centered on finding comfort and convenience through our perpetual search for pleasure. To be sincere in your own introspection and self-work means becoming more conscious of how you are transforming energy.

Many people are super conscious about cleaning their house or car, but neglect their own being with excessiveness and artificial pollutants. If we were simply to eat more organic and natural fresh foods, shut down the computer, throw away the television, and sell the mobile phone, we would discover a more aware state of consciousness that is not disturbed by those aspects of our life that distract us from our center. The body is the temple of the eternal spirit, and it is about time that we treat it as such. Our level of attunement depends on how we transform energy, and this is significant if we want to experience enlightenment now. Attunement is a response to how energy is transformed. It is actually the fragrance of energy itself.

The source at the divine ground of our being is disconnected because we bombard our nine gates with artificiality rather than nature. When we begin to refine our consciousness, that perennial connection to the source of our being is slowly reestablished. This happens because that connection is an outcome of energetic attunement. Attunement is in essence a signal and transducer of energy.

To articulate this we can use a satellite dish as an analogy. When we are looking for the signal from the satellite to our satellite dish, if we point our dish in the wrong direction then there will be no signal and the television screen will show only static. But if we find the signal way out there in space, then the picture on the screen becomes clear. Similarly, in order for us to attune ourselves to the source of all things then our attention must be pointed in the right direction, which is within. If we make that connection then our level of attunement will reveal the transparency and reflectivity of our consciousness. With this connection we attune at a different level. But keep in mind that everyone is always connected to the source, but the clouds of artificiality obscure the clear blue sky, blocking the signal of one's level of attunement.

Attunement is needed if you are to discover enlightenment. Attunement brings our time-bound understandings of enlightenment out of isolation and into a greater recognition of energy and consciousness.

Many sages may get confused as to why some individuals truly "get it" and others don't. Some individuals truly feel the sense of unity and marinate their soul in the irreducible essence, which makes them genuinely humble. Some sages do overlook this attunement aspect of our consciousness, not out of ignorance, but simply because outside of the research of the ancient metaphysicians there has not been a lot of knowledge on the function of energy and attunement.

In the modern era, with the advent of new sciences that mimic the great metaphysicians of Hermeticism, Gnosticism, and Vedanta, our question should be why do some people attune to a higher frequency than others? Fundamentally we cannot say without getting into speculation. For example, sometimes we may say someone has an "old soul." Intuitively we may feel this sense of their being wise beyond their human age, but it is far too vague to attribute it to attunement. We can, however, explore how energy functions in relation to attunement and the methods people take to refine their consciousness.

THE RHYTHM AND VIBRATION OF CONSCIOUSNESS

Two of the principles that make up the energy and consciousness of the universe are rhythm and vibration. Yet we cannot separate energy from consciousness, as they are both comingled. For the sake of this discussion we will use the word *energy*. Attunement, as we said, is a signal and transducer of energy. To understand this we need to realize how vibration and rhythm are modulated.

The physical, mental, and spiritual planes of consciousness are not separate and are in harmonious rhythm from a higher level of attunement. For vibration and rhythm to coalesce and for an individual to reach a higher level of attunement, we need to comprehend that when we talk about signals we have to acknowledge the existence of frequency. When we mention frequency we can use the analogy of a radio. When we are trying to pick up a signal on a radio we have to finely tune it to receive the signal clearly. When the signal is picked up clearly then the rhythm of song is heard beautifully. The vibratory frequency condenses its vibration to a level of tuning that gives rise to a latent rhythm within the structure of the frequency. The rhythm was eclipsed until the fine tuning found the frequency where the signal originates. Rhythm becomes more awe-inspiring when the vibration latent within it begins to raise its velocity, and this can only rise when the frequency of the signal is received more clearly.

This analogy is in direct relationship to a human being, as we are also energy. Our attunement when refined will pick up a frequency from the source of all being located within us, and then the harmonious vibration and rhythm of our perception and understanding will become transparent. With radio, there is one satellite and many different frequencies. And as with a human being there is one source—call it Brahman, Tao, God, Allah, or what have you—and there are different frequencies to which we attune our being. For example, someone who is perpetually caught in the details of worldly affairs is at a low level of attunement because they cannot receive the signal coming from the source clearly, as is evidenced through their separatist mode of consciousness. Their attunement is distorted and blurry, and so from no awareness of the signal they act in a disconnected manner.

Yet let's be mindful that different frequencies and levels of attunement do not mean one is better or worse, as that is only a subjective judgment according to the individual. It may mean that our actions are the result of ignorance, but deep down all levels of perceptual attunement are necessary to build the fabric of reality. We cannot have the background with no foreground, the order without chaos.

When our consciousness has cleansed itself from the distractions and toxins that distort our view of reality, we come to realize that there is no truth in the monarchical view, as the refined mind that has reached an attuned wisdom of the universe equates purely to perception and understanding. Problems arise only when people attempt to prove that they have a higher-level attunement, which is actually evidence that they still have a low level of attunement, as their mind is still bound by ignorance. In the modern era a lot of people proclaim to be enlightened, which is a dead giveaway of prevalent latent separatist tendencies, and the evidence that one is still under the magical spell of the monarchical view of reality. One who is truly at a high level of attunement is directly connected to the source, and their consciousness is so refined and subtle that it affects the whole energetic field of the universe without having any intention to do so.

When the Atman is clearly revealed to be Brahman then the microcosm becomes the macrocosm in function and being. This means that one is no longer just an "effect" but has now become a "cause" and the emanation of the source of Brahman energy. We may think of the source as radiating extraordinary light into our manifest world, but one who has united with the source, a sage for example, begins to illuminate the world through their humble wisdom and beingness. A being of this magnitude becomes like the glow of the sun in our celestial sphere, except it is the central sun of the irreducible essence that illuminates their consciousness. The vibration of one in this high level of attunement affects the universal field of energy and brings a certain harmonious, tranquil rhythm to the world. Attunement is an aspect of the energetic experiential realm that most do not consider and are hardly conscious of.

ATTUNEMENT TO AURAS

The modern era of science is beginning to understand this field of research concerning energy and attunement. The late scientist Valerie Hunt did remarkable research on the energetic phenomena of auras. Best known for her pioneering research in the field of bioenergy, she broke much ground on the subject of subtle energy that most cannot physically perceive. In regard to auras, she found that some people can perceive the colorful auras around a human, which allows them to discern an individual's level of attunement. But because this ability is isolated to a few people, the masses are skeptical. Hunt discovered, using electromyography (EMG), a device and technique used for evaluating and recording electrical activity produced by our skeletal muscles, that this method can also pick up the electrical presence of the human energy field. The frequency of auras and an individual's attunement can be measured through color coding as a result. Michael Talbot explains Hunt's findings in his book *The Holographic Universe*:

> The normal frequency range of the electrical activity in the brain is
> between 0 and 100 cycles per second (cps), with most of the activity
> occurring between 0 and 30 cps. Muscle frequency goes up to about

225 cps, and the heart goes up to about 250 cps, but this is where electrical activity associated with biological function drops off. In addition to these, Hunt discovered that the electrodes of the electromyography could pick up another field of energy radiating from the body, much subtler and smaller in amplitude than the traditionally recognized body electricities but with frequencies that averaged between 100 and 1600 cps, and which sometimes went even higher. Moreover, instead of emanating from the brain, heart, or muscles, the field was strongest in the areas of the body associated with the chakras. . . .

One of Hunt's most startling findings is that certain talents and abilities seem to be related to the presence of specific frequencies in a person's energy field. She has found that when the main focus of a person's consciousness is on the material world, the frequencies of their energy field tend to be in the lower range and are not too far removed from the 250 cps of the body's biological frequencies. In addition to this, people who are psychic or who have healing abilities also have frequencies of roughly 400 to 800 cps in their field. . . .

People who have frequencies above 900 cps are what Hunt calls mystical personalities. . . . They are aware of the cosmic interrelatedness of all things and are in touch with every level of human experience. They are anchored in ordinary reality, but often have both psychic and trance abilities. However, their frequencies also extend way beyond the bands associated with these capabilities. Using a modified electromyogram (an electromyogram can normally detect frequencies only up to 20,000 cps) Hunt has encountered individuals who have frequencies as high as 200,000 cps in their energy fields. This is intriguing, for mystical traditions have often referred to highly spiritual individuals as possessing a "higher vibration" than normal people.[4]

This may give the skeptics some hard evidence, and is only one example of many. But for those who really experience a heightened level of attunement there is no need for proof, as they live it. These higher levels of attunement are not isolated to a sage because we all have this higher state of consciousness latent within us. But as with the radio, we need to tune our being to the source of the signal, and there are numerous methods to do so.

A human being, in a sense, is analogous to an antenna in this regard, as methods elevate our consciousness. The most tried and true methods of attunement are ancient spiritual practices: hatha yoga, t'ai chi, qigong, pranayama, meditation, and so on, all methods of attuning oneself to the irreducible essence. As we become sincere in self-work then that feeling within that is beyond words begins to grow more intimate with our being. The biggest problem with those people using any method is we become attracted only to the method rather than its objective. As a result we postpone our enlightenment to become better at the method in the same way a gymnast wants to refine her performance so it looks nice to others.

We need to be mindful that in sincere self-work a method of attunement is not itself a facilitator of enlightenment. Methods are purely medicinal for our ills, not dietary. The function of a method is to attune your perception and understanding to the nature of reality. It is a door into realizing that enlightenment is right now. The internal peaceful life of those ancient masters is the prerogative, and a method is a cure to our conditioned hypnosis that blocks this awareness.

When we do attune our being to the spiritual level of the source of reality, we begin to hear the song of the universe and also perceive the universe for the first time as it truly *is*. Hearing the song of the universe is to clearly hear intuition, where our individual and divine will merge as one. Mental virtue is born as a result, known in Sanskrit as *dharma* (धर्म) and Chinese as *te* (德)* where our virtue brings the

---

*In Chinese *te* can mean power or virtue depending on how it is used. *Dharma* is an inclusive word that can mean duty, mission, law, the Buddha's teaching, and virtue. In classical texts the two terms are often used interchangeably.

presence of eternity into the world of manifestation, usually facilitated through art. In a sense, we come into chorus with the universe and inspire others as a result of virtue.

Attunement in this regard is definitely a musical thing, where we ascend in scale but are never excluded from the other notes. This also relates to our perception, where the very act of seeing cannot be fixed indefinitely on either the foreground or the background, as it is in accord with rhythm and acts in the same manner as breathing. When we are in accord with this perceptual rhythm, we begin to perceive the existence of the universe as it *is* through the involution (the perception caught in the details of life, the foreground, and so on) and evolution of consciousness. When a sage's consciousness is highly attuned, she perceives eternity in the manifest world in the ever-present moment. In my book *The Science and Practice of Humility*, I explain the essence of what we believe is a reality based on dualistic opposites:

Duality is based on the theory that if you have good, then there must be bad, meaning that everything has its opposite. For example, we have the two poles of cold and hot, light and dark, being and non-being, microcosm and macrocosm, and so on. We know one cannot exist without the other; we need dark to know light, hot to know cold, and so on. Where does the light end and the dark begin? Does either have a definite ending or are they part of a continuous stream? All of these apparent opposites are in fact the same thing, differing only in degree. Just as a musical scale starts with C and moves up the scale in a continuous fashion until it reaches another C, the nature of duality between any two poles is an aspect of rhythm and vibration expressing itself in the manifest world.

In each area of consideration, such as good and bad or light and dark, the degree of separation between the poles is determined by an individual's psychology, which varies according to the individual's conditioning. When the masses see duality in the world, they are only trying to interpret the polarity they have created in their mind.[5]

There is an order to the chaotic patterns of duality within the three planes of consciousness. Attuning to enlightenment, to the here and now, clears our perception to perceive this order. This perception is the true meaning behind the "vision of God." A sage's enlightened attunement is this vision.

8
The Pattern and Order
of Universal Consciousness

AT A HIGHER LEVEL of attunement there is an intrinsic order to the universe. Enlightenment is an awareness that perceives this order. Grounded in this vision, a sage does not seek to change life because life is always changing on a subtle level to the movements of rhythm and vibration. Life is always as it *is* through the eyes of enlightenment. To try to change any piece of this universal riddle would be to imply that we do not trust life because we feel alien to the universe. Resting in the "jewel of the lotus flower,"* a sage perceives a pattern and order to all things in the universe; no matter whether we assume it is good or bad, the order and pattern are there. As the great Taoist sage Chuang-tzu said, "When there is no more separation between 'this' and 'that,' it is called the still-point of the Tao. At the still-point in the center of the circle one can see the infinite in all things."[1]

Listening to these words of Chuang-tzu may not have any meaning to those people with a low level of attunement, as it is not something tangible we can physically show to prove its reality. A sage's higher level of attunement is purely experiential existing in the very act of perceiv-

---

*This is the mani mantra, *om mani padme hum*. This mantra expresses that dedication to practicing a path that recognizes an indivisible union between method and wisdom can transform your impure body, speech, and mind into the pure body, speech, and mind of a Buddha.

ing and intuitive understanding. Both perception and intuition are discarded in our highly intellectual world, blind to the interconnected unfoldment and latent unity of all things. Those with a low level of attunement will perceive only separation between apparent opposites because their consciousness is fixed on the dramas of life. We should not assume, though, that a sage is above being human, as humans are both mountains and valleys, a concept that Carl Jung explains in his commentary on Richard Wilhelm's translation of *The Secret of the Golden Flower:*

> What, on a lower level, had led to the wildest conflicts and to panicky outbursts of emotion, viewed from the higher level of the personality, now seemed like a storm in the valley seen from a high mountain-top. This does not mean that the thunderstorm is robbed of its reality, but instead of being in it, one is now above it. However, since we are both valley and mountain with respect to the psyche, it might seem a vain illusion to feel oneself beyond what is human. One certainly does feel the affect and is shaken and tormented by it, yet at the same time one is aware of a higher consciousness, which prevents one from becoming identical with the affect, a consciousness which takes the affect objectively, and can say, "I know that I suffer."[2]

One reason sages can be hard to understand is because the masses are accustomed to the habit of judging or belittling mystical matters, as the majority's consciousness is constantly distracted. How could we trust anyone's perception of reality if they constantly stimulate their mind with vain entertainment, materialism, and excessive thinking? One in such a state acts as if hypnotized and in dire need of a sage's wisdom. If they are humble enough, they might even seek out such wisdom. But our level of attunement will always be at a low level so long as we attempt to perceive reality through the mental filters of all the distractions of our society and culture. If we have a higher level of attunement, we perceive a pattern and order to the universe because we've begun the process of emptying our mind of all its unnecessary garbage. Cleaning the filter that obscures our perception elevates our attunement to reality.

Society, culture, and religion teach us a distracted perspective of reality based on dualism. God and man are separate, nature and man are separate, female and male are separate, the earth and the sun are separate, and so on. This dualism naturally leads to monarchical thinking. We are blind to the source because of this low level of attunement. This is why many people laugh at the reality of a pattern and order to this universe that we can all experience through our consciousness. This is not a problem, however, as it has been with us since the dawn of humanity. The mystical perception of the universal pattern and order is usually thought of as a sage's vision, yet the ancient masters brought this perception out of pure experience and into the realm of the manifest.

BRAHMAN BORN IN RITUAL AND LIBERATED IN LIFE

The Dravidian civilization of the Indus Valley, an area that extends from northeast Afghanistan to Pakistan and northwest India, thrived for about one thousand years from 2500 to 1500 BCE, and it is suggested that this civilization could have been far older than these generally accepted dates. The two main cities of the Dravidian civilization were Mohenjo-daro and Harappa, which were amazingly both brick cities with extraordinary sanitary arrangements, sewage systems, wells, and so on. The cities were laid out in a mechanical fashion in a very simple order.

When these cities were excavated in the 1920s archeologists found no temples, but they did find an enormous communal bath. This bath is significant considering the religious tradition of India has at its core a spiritual practice of bathing daily, especially in the mother Ganga (that is, the Ganges River), along the *ghats* (embankments made in steps of stone slabs along the river bank where pilgrims perform ritual ablutions) of Varanasi (also known as Benares or Kashi). This continuity of bathing as a spiritual practice goes back far before the holy Vedas were written down, which is believed to be around 1000 BCE, with many scholars suggesting that they could be far older.

These discoveries point to a civilization primarily focused on spiritual contemplation and social harmony rather than religious doctrine and devotion from a monarchical perspective of society. One of the only pieces of art from the Dravidians that we have discovered is the Pashupati (Lord of the Animals) Seal found in Mohenjo-daro in 1928 or 1929, dating from 2600 to 1900 BCE. The Pashupati Seal (see figure 8.1) depicts a seated yogi in contemplation, which is an Indian motif that is not found anywhere else in those ancient times. This piece of art points to a civilization focused on individual self-work and the mystical realm of the mind.

Figure 8.1. The Pashupati Seal

Around 1500 BCE the contemplative tradition of the Dravidians was changed forever when the Aryans came sweeping in from the north. The invasion by the Aryans transformed life in general for the Dravidian people, who strived for equanimity within society and were people of trade and agriculture. But the Aryans brought the monarchical idea of the ruling castes, the Brahmins (the magician-priest class) and the Kshatriyas (the nobility or warrior class). These two classes go together and represent the conquering tradition of the Aryans. As a result of this invasion, we have a two-tier system with the Aryan Brahmins and Kshatriyas on top, and the Dravidian Vaishyas (merchants and farmers) and Shudras (laborers and peasants) on the bottom of the social order. On top of new social structure, the Aryans brought along with them ritual sacrifice, which may have come from Greek sacrificial rituals, as the Aryans are the cousins of the Dorian and Achaean Greeks, whom we know from the time of Homer. The sacrificial ritual was the primary, and maybe only, spiritual practice of the Aryan priesthood.

The Aryan Brahmins developed a series of hymns to coincide with the magic and mystery of these sacrificial rituals. These hymns that were sung during rituals were in fact the sacred texts of the Vedas. The singing of the Vedic hymns in the ritual of sacrifice was thought to address the Indian gods. Before the Aryans formulated the Vedas into hymns that were written down, they were part of a mysterious oral tradition among the Dravidian people and were preserved with the help of elaborate mnemonic techniques that somehow contain an immense power. This power may be why the Aryan Brahmins thought of the Vedas as the "song of the universe." The reason they believed this is because when the Vedas were sung in correspondence to an animal sacrifice to the gods, they perceived an order and pattern to their ritual, which was charged by an immense presence of a divine energy felt by all who attended.

The energy felt and perceived in sacrifice was called Brahman. This concept of Brahman is the same that we have already mentioned, which we have referred to in relation to Tao, God, Allah, Universe, and so on. The idea of Brahman may have occurred first in relation to ritual sacrifice. But we can only speculate about this because there is no extensive knowledge about older civilizations to assume otherwise. Nevertheless, the manipulation of the instruments of sacrifice was a magical and transformative process. The *Brahmanas* are a set of texts that interpret the Vedas in this way and are elaborate theological "stage directions" in relation to the sacred hymns. The awareness of Brahman in ritual brought about strict etiquette with the priesthood. Everything had to be perfect when performing sacrifices, as it was a way of communicating with the divine Brahman, a correspondence between the microcosm and macrocosm. So there was an impulse to perform sacrifices precisely so as not to be rude to the source of all life.

The awareness of the order and pattern of Brahman in sacrifice led to the belief that there is a certain structured order to society. The Hindu Indian caste system has its birth in this idea. As I mentioned, the Aryans made up the Brahmins and Kshatriyas, who controlled the lower two castes of the Vaishyas and Shudras made up of the native Dravidians.

This type of social order is not isolated to the Indus Valley, as the Chinese sage Confucius thought the Tao (Brahman) existed in the manufacturing of a social order. But the flaw of both the Aryans and Confucius was that this social order was fit only for the priesthood and nobility. Fit for a king, we could say. It always has a bias toward the monarchy of society, culture, and religion. The reason for this bias is obvious when you consider that both in the Aryan civilization and in China the structured performance of ritual, sacrifice, and ancestor worship is thought to be the only place where the divine energy and radiance of Brahman exists. They thought that if they could set up a social order that functioned as a type of sacrifice to the gods, then the energy of Brahman would come through this caste system.

Yet this social system is designed by the upper two castes without any consideration for the common people. How could we design a social system in alignment with Brahman without the input of the whole population? We couldn't because a decision based on a monarchical view of reality is fundamentally flawed and out of sync with how the energy of Brahman naturally expresses itself.

One of the main problems in the implementation of the caste system of the Vedic civilization, and still a problem within our current world, is that the cosmic order of Brahman is thought of in concrete terms coming from its conceptual birth in sacrifice. Because of the ritual of sacrifice, the priesthood believed that there is a structure to follow that builds the energy of Brahman, as if it exists outside of the universe. And in the same way that the Brahmins could feel and sense the energy of Brahman in sacrifice, they believed that everybody would sense it in the caste system, as the castes themselves were thought to be a structure built as a bridge between this world and the mystical realm.

Both the sacrifice and the caste system are a collective point of view. The Aryans always emphasized a collective perspective rather than the individual contemplation of the Dravidians. As a result people began to confuse the alignment to cosmic order with social function. People were made to believe that, by following their social duty according to their allotted caste, they could bring the irreducible essence into the world. The individual is discarded in favor of the collective ideal of morality. And yet, morality itself is an illusion because its meaning differs from individual to individual.

This collective ideal of morality is prevalent in the East because it is thought that if you sacrifice, or crucify, your ego to the needs of society and caste then you will be emanating the Brahman into the world. In this sense you "are" your caste and duty and nothing else. This is supposed to medicate our individual desires and temptations that usually harm others and ourselves. This social philosophy also suppresses an individual's nature of self-expression. Even though this perspective originated in ancient Asia, it is still subtly with us in the modern era both in the East and West.

CONFORMITY AND NONCONFORMITY
IN ANCIENT INDIA

The collective view is esoterically known as "the right-hand path of conformity" and the view of natural individuality is known as "the left-hand path of nonconformity" through self-expression. The right-hand path suits the priesthood (Brahmins) and nobility (Kshatriyas) of any society, but not the rest because the majority are treated as mere slaves who should conform to society and the will of the upper castes. The right-hand path of any age moves the focus away from individual self-work and contemplation to external worship and idolatry, because the Brahman is thought to be perceived only in individual sacrifice to the collective. As a result we are taught to align with social duty and obligations rather than following our bliss, as Joseph Campbell would say.

The Aryans were shortsighted because the fundamental basis of any group structure is the individual. The individual is the seed of the society. The society is the outcome of the individual, not the other way around. But our modern world is still built on the Aryans' back-to-front social ideology that the individual is the product of society. The assumption that the individual is the product of a society results from the monarchical view of reality. We are indoctrinated to bow unquestionably to a society, culture, and religion as one would to a king. But the fundamental nature of reality is the individual, and they are who make society. Any group itself is an abstraction, because the group is only a notion that individuals agree upon. Social harmony will never be achieved by our attempts to muzzle the individual through rules and regulations that repress their spiritual nature.

Real social harmony and peace will come to fruition only when the individual is trusted to follow her own nature and life path. That can occur only when the upper echelons of society, and even the average individual, stop telling people how to live their lives. When we sincerely look within, our conditioned agendas for the world will diminish. But this is impossible if we are not sincere about our individual self-work and contemplation. So long as we have an agenda, we will continue to try to impose our will on the world. As the individual *is* the society, these personal agendas become social systems of control, such as the caste system. Social conformity and a gross lack of critical thinking becomes the life of the average individual as a result.

Everything becomes externalized, as we believe any form of hierarchy has power, and we, individuals, do not. This was the Aryan viewpoint of the cosmic energy and order of Brahman. The performance of sacrifice was the only way to Brahman. And this sense of Brahman was only for the initiated, not the general public. This idea that Brahman was isolated to sacrifice and the caste system eventually had to crumble and change over time, and so, too, does our current social structure.

THE FOREST PHILOSOPHERS

Around the eighth century BCE came the heretical movement of the forest philosophers, known as *vanaprastha* in Sanskrit. The forest philosophers, and maybe also some already initiated Brahmins, began to perceive and understand that the energy of the sacrifice, Brahman, was in all life. As a result of this movement, the great texts of India, the Upanishads, came into existence. These forest philosophers, sages if you will, not only intuitively perceived Brahman in sacrifice and social order, but also in the unfolding of a flower, the movement of clouds, the seasons, our relationships, our thinking, matter, and so on.

The difference between the forest philosophers and the upper two castes of the Aryans is that the performance of sacrifice and the caste system are merely intellectual, meaning that both are contrived for control. The forest philosophers, on the other hand, intuitively know that trying to control life means not truly knowing Brahman, as the irreducible essence is felt within our consciousness when we trust the process of the universe.

These revolutionary sages of those ancient times would say there is nothing to do in order to know or be one with the cosmic order of Brahman. No ritual is needed. The upper two castes of the Aryans brought in the external significance of control into the Dravidian civilization. The Dravidians went from a contemplative society, as we see with the Pashupati Seal, to a community dependent on going to a temple to commit idolatry. But with the arrival of the heretical movement of the forest philosophers of the eighth century BCE, the pre-Aryan, Dravidian mysticism began an intermarriage with the Aryan beliefs in a sort of renaissance of the earlier tradition. After eight hundred years in India, the political power of the Aryans began to lose its force and authority. A mixing of the two cultures took place that reshaped India and the world forever.

The resurgence of the earlier Dravidian tradition brought about this transformation. When the concept of Brahman left the confines of ritual and entered into all universal life, a shift from Aryan sacrifice back to Dravidian contemplation took place. The movement from external worship to individual self-work brought a whole new sphere of culture.

In India you can still perceive the remnants of this mixing through Hinduism, as it is superficially represented by external worship but grounded in individual contemplation through Vedanta. Those rebellious forest philosophers of the eighth century BCE understood how the world-affirming perspective of the Aryans and the world renouncing ways of the Dravidians are mutual and interdependent philosophies. In some arcane way, they complement each other, which the forest philosophers discovered. They realized that renouncing the world is really an affirmation of the world because you trust it. If the ancient axiom of "All is Brahman and I am That" is correct, how could we not trust life in its complete spectrum of light and sound? This paradox that renunciation spawns affirmation is prevalent in the Taoist wisdom of China. In Richard Wilhelm's translation and commentary of the I Ching he states:

Not every man has an obligation to mingle in the affairs of the world. There are some who are developed to such a degree that they are justified in letting the world go its own way and in refusing to enter public life with a view of reforming it. But this does not imply a right to remain idle or to sit back and merely criticize. Such withdrawal is justified only when we strive to realize in ourselves the higher aims of mankind. For although the sage remains distant from the turmoil of daily life, he creates incomparable human values for the future.[3]

The mystical consciousness of a sage slowly came back into the consciousness of the masses. Contemplation regained its place, as individual spirituality took precedence over social duty. The whole mixing of Aryan and Dravidian cultures was meant to be, as this was a part of the cosmic order. The forest philosophers recognized this from their deep contemplation. The Aryans brought the intellectual sphere into the intuitive sphere of the Dravidians and vice versa. Without each other, both the intellect and intuition are out of balance. The marriage of both brought about a higher level of attunement, which opens the inner gates to enlightenment. The esoteric terminology of this marriage in the wisdom traditions is known as the *intellectual intuition* (a subtle state of consciousness and perception as mentioned earlier). The intellectual intuition gave a cognition and perception of Brahman at greater depths in reality for those forest philosophers.

THE PATTERN OF BRAHMAN IN TIME, SCRIPTURE, ARCHAEOLOGY, AND CELESTIAL BODIES

As we see a sacred geometrical pattern within a sunflower, the forest philosophers could perceive an encoded pattern and message in the human instruments of civilization, nature's process, and in the greater universe. They discovered that there is a pattern to consciousness perceived by one resting in the attunement of enlightenment. There is a cosmic order flowing through the mind of an individual who is enlightened in the now. This pattern comes through the enlightened mind without any intention to seek it out. People make the mistake of assuming that when this pattern is found in the creations of human-kind that the individuals who brought them into manifestation some-how planned the divine patterns that we discover. This assumption, again, isolates us from nature.

Art is integral to the essence of human nature, just as aroma is integral to the essence of a flower's nature. When we don't plan or con-trol life our artistic essence naturally arises in our mind spontaneously. This is why the greatest and most timeless art was never planned, as it just happened of its own accord. In Chinese this spontaneous nature is known as *tzu-jan*, which I mentioned earlier. Extraordinary art is not self-conscious, in the same way that the best athletes are not self-conscious in their extraordinary performances. A higher power within the unconscious takes over the reins and our ego just becomes a passive passenger in the process of truly inspired art.

It is amazing that when someone produces a beautiful piece of art, if you ask them to do it again they begin to think about it and pro-duce something that could not even stand in the shadow of the original piece. The dharma, virtue of our inner world, can only shine through our being when we are in the immediate moment. When we think of past or future, we invariably get in the way of letting the cosmic order shine through our being. When our ego is out of the way, the trace of the pattern of Brahman is left behind for the enlightened to intuit, like a divine map that we follow into the garden of our heart, where our perception can see Brahman in all life.

The calculations of esoteric students and spiritual seekers reveal some startling findings in relation to Brahman in all life. This goes back to the Vedic civilization of the Aryans and Dravidians. In the scriptures and time systems of the Vedic civilization we perceive a cos-mic order that is an attempt to map the irreducible essence, Brahman. In the very first Veda of four, known as the Rig Veda, we discover a verse that appears to have no relevance to modern civilization:

So let the Brahman hear the praise we utter.
This hath the four-horned Buffalo emitted.
Four are his horns,
three are the feet that bear him;
his heads are two,
his hands are seven in number.[4]

This verse is significant in understanding the pattern and order of universal consciousness. The Rig Veda, esoteric though it may appear, is actually a description of the universe, that is, Brahman. This verse is a map of the cycles of consciousness and time that Hindus refer to as the *yugas*, which I mentioned briefly earlier. There are two systems of the yugas: an ancient long-count map, and a more recent short-count map. Both are based on the *kalpa,* a Sanskrit word from Hindu and Buddhist cosmology that means "aeon." One kalpa, in the ancient system, equals 4.32 billion years as described in the ancient texts of the Puranas, especially the Vishnu Purana and Bhagavata Purana. This long-count system of one kalpa, which is of our concern in relation to the Rig Veda, is made up of one thousand *maha-yugas,* that is, "great yugas." The duration of a maha-yuga is built on a system of four yugas, which make up a complex world-age doctrine that maps the cycles of change and consciousness.

Satya (ideal or truthful) *Yuga* (1,728,000 years)
Treta (virtue declined by a quarter) *Yuga* (1,296,000 years)
Dvapara (virtue reduced by half) *Yuga* (864,000 years)
Kali (virtue reduced to a quarter) *Yuga* (432,000 years)

All of these numbers relate to the above verse from the Rig Veda. In the Rig Veda we perceive a direct relationship with one kalpa. When we break down the age of one kalpa we reveal a numeric correlation to the Rig Veda. One kalpa is 4,320,000,000 years. "Four are his horns," 4. "Three are the feet that bear him," 3. "His heads are two," 2. "His hands are seven in number," 0,000,000. Though the majority of people would never make this connection, a sage on a higher level of attunement recognizes the pattern. The Rig Veda lays it out directly in our face. Yet, if our intellectual intuition has not developed, the Rig Veda is merely mysterious words and has no relationship to the yugas. The evidence of this cosmic order of Brahman is there for all of us to see.

But what is the significance of this correlation between the Rig Veda and one kalpa? Both describe the earth as an aspect of Brahman. The energy of Brahman is everything that makes up the earth. One kalpa, 4.32 billion years, refers to the age of the earth. The relationship of the earth to Brahman is thus described in the Rig Veda. But keep in mind that the author of the Rig Veda did not intend to match our modern measurements as it would have been impossible to know future calculations of time, distance, etc. The mystery is therefore the correlation we discover between the Rig Veda and our modern measurements, which are completely isolated from each other by thousands of years.

These numbers not only correspond to the age of the earth; the Kali Yuga is 432,000 years, an even fraction of one kalpa, for example. But these numbers also stretch into the makeup of the two celestial bodies that give us direct life on earth. We discover a fractal order of numbers in the ages and material structure of the earth, sun, and moon from the Rig Veda and the yugas.

When we look into the material structure of the sun, we discover that the radius is 432,000 miles (measured at 432,450 miles according to the Solar and Heliospheric Observatory (SOHO) spacecraft during 2003 and 2006) and the diameter is therefore 864,000 miles (which should be approximately 846,900 miles if the SOHO spacecraft is accurate but other research speculates the sun's diameter to be about 865,374 miles). Remarkably, this correlates to the Kali and Dvapara Yugas, as well as our modern scale of time, as one day is 86,400 seconds and half a day is 43,200 seconds. There is, therefore a direct connection between the sun and the Vedic map of time, our current map of time, and scripture.

On top of this startling discovery, the moon has a diameter of

2,160 miles, which is 200 times smaller than the radius of the sun. The radius of the moon is therefore 1,080 miles, which is a significant spiritual number. In the wisdom traditions 108 is known as a lunar number. It is also the atomic weight of silver, which is the metal commonly associated with the moon and the lunar aspect. As it is a lunar number, 108 is related to human beings because we are lunar beings to the solar light within, because our life rises and falls in the same way that the moon illuminates and then moves into darkness. In many religions we see that 108 is encoded into the ornaments and temples of worship. The sacred beads of many religious traditions, known as *rudraksha mala* in Sanskrit, from the rudraksha tree, are 108 in number, which may have originated in the Vedic civilization.

In relation to the human being, the 108 sacred beads are used for meditation and prayer. On average when an individual goes into meditation, where a deep cleansing breath corresponds to one bead, it usually takes 43 minutes to complete a full 108-bead inhale-exhale breathing process, which should put you in a deep state of silence beyond the senses. These numbers also correspond to reciting mantras with the 108 beads. This process of 108 to go beyond the senses amazingly relates to the structure of the number. The number 108 is made up of 9 x 12. The number 12 represents the twelve signs of the zodiac, and 9 represents the nine gates of the human being, as we discussed earlier (see pages 55 and 102). The 43 minutes it takes to go beyond the nine gates also relates to the number of one kalpa. In a fractal harmony we discover a resonance from divine scripture all the way through the phenomena of the universe down into a human being.

The encoded message in the Rig Veda also relates to the human experience. There are four yugas that define our consciousness, three planes of consciousness that build our reality, two feminine and masculine principles of the psyche and life, and seven chakras that build our psycho-energetic being. This is a direct connection between the human microcosm and the macrocosm of Brahman, which came through the minds of those who created the Vedas.

The art of dharma that emanates through our being is a language of the Divine, for those with a higher level of attunement to perceive the script within life. The Great Pyramid of Giza is one of the best examples outside of the Vedas in regard to this divine language. In fact, the very numbers encoded in the Vedas are significant in relation to the Great Pyramid. For example, if we are to use the J. H. Cole calculation of the Great Pyramid's height (480.953 feet) including the socle at the base of the pyramid (21.6535 inches), we have a height of 482.7575 feet. If we are to multiply that height by an even fraction of the sacred number of one kalpa, which is 43,200, we discover this number 20,855,124 feet, which is 3,949.834 miles. When we compare this number to the World Geodetic System 1972 of the Earth's polar radius, which is 3,949.8934 miles, there is amazingly a difference of only 313 feet between both measurements. The Great Pyramid of Giza is essentially a scale model of the Earth according to these numbers. The scale model of the Great Pyramid is of one hemisphere at a ratio of 1:43,200. In his book *Pyramid Odyssey,* William R. Fix states:

> The history of man may be far longer and stranger than we think. The Great Pyramid may indeed not fit in with what we believe about the past and the nature of the world. Thousands of years ago someone measured the earth with remarkable accuracy and recorded this information in the dimensions of the largest and possibly the oldest stone building on our planet.[5]

Either intentionally or purely by chance, the Great Pyramid is a scale model of the earth and is in correspondence with the cosmic order of numbers that are found within the Vedic culture. This megalithic structure is one of the grandest pieces of art in our world, and it could not have come into existence without a mind that received its image within the immediate moment with no preplanning. Once the image was received in the mind's eye, an enormous process of unfoldment began.

The construction of the Great Pyramid, and the unfoldment of any art, holds an esoteric key to enlightenment. Though we receive art spontaneously now, there is a process of unfoldment to reveal this latent cosmic order within the manifest world; art's message can bear fruit only within a journey. The macrocosmic pattern and order of Brahman can only be understood through the microcosmic journey of a human being. The cosmic order and pattern of Brahman is perceived in reality for the universal purpose of unraveling the riddle we call our lives. Unraveling this riddle brings us into harmony with Brahman. Enlightenment is the fruit of this harmony, and as the artist knows that their dharma is the union of spontaneity and unfoldment, so too do those of a higher level of attunement know that enlightenment is the union of now and the journey.

9

The Journey Is the Destination and the Destination Is the Journey

HARMONIZING WITH THE COSMIC PATTERN and order of the universe is sometimes thought of in the sense of a journey. We devise maps to traverse eternity. Eternity is mistakenly thought of as some place in the far-off distance. Our focus becomes a destination that is an eternal realm in the future, that is, heaven. As a result, the journey to this destination becomes secondary and almost an impediment to our spiritual growth. In this approach we miss out on all of the wonderful experiences that we call our life due to our focus on the far distant future.

We build mental prisons for ourselves from which we will be set free at a future date or when death comes. We lock ourselves into home mortgages, loans for material possessions, and also a postponement of enlightenment so that we can start "really" living our life sometime in the future. This tendency assumes that we are not already free as we are now. Our society, culture, and religions all promote this attitude, but ultimately there is no one to blame other than yourself. We build all the authorities we accept in our mind.

The prisons that we lock ourselves into are based on the authorities we accept. Enlightenment is imprisoned with these beliefs. Most of the maps that are created for us in life are confused with the territory, as Alfred Korzybski exposed (see page 96). In the context of enlightenment, most of our maps explain that this eternal consciousness is somewhere way off in the distance, and in some cases a place after death. We are taught to practice to become, refine to perceive, and so on. Though these may be necessary to our understanding, the problem is that all our attention points to a destination in some state that we assume is not innate to our being. But as we have discussed in this book, eternity is not a long time away because it is of no time, and so it must be right here with you reading these words. Most of the spiritual maps we use, that is, doctrines, confuse eternity with time.

The human concept of time contributes to this confusion. All systems of time we have created are based on an attempt to map eternity, and in some sense we have done a good job at this when we consider the yugas or astrology.

The problem arises when we begin to think that the systems of time we have created *are* eternity. Remember, eternity is outside of time and a map. Any calculations of time, as well as any scripture that explains eternity, are only symbols. We identify too often with the symbol. Spiritually we are vexed by this problem because we get caught up with intellectualizing whether we are overcompensating for the map or symbol, or if we even understand what the map is referring to.

We become split into two spiritual groups as a result. One group resonates only with the path, and so are ardent practitioners, while the other is focused on the immediate moment and are attempting to yoke enlightenment to every moment of life. Neither group is wrong in their approach, but rather they are wrong in their dissociation with the other. The first group separates the journey from the goal, while the second group separates the goal from the journey. Understanding the nature of reality turns into a tug-of-war between both perspectives. The battle between the intellectual understanding that we are on a journey versus the intuitive understanding that we are already home right here and now continues to rage on in the mind of the spiritually inclined. To attempt to hold on to one perspective over the other divides our perception of the universe and its natural process.

THE INTERPLAY OF UNIFIED OPPOSITES

These divided perspectives isolate the universe to a single dimension: either all journey or only destination. We attempt, in both perspectives, to discern reality by not observing nature as it *is* because our psychological filters obscure our clarity.

In the Taoist tradition of China, which spawned from the ancient sage Lao-tzu, the nature of reality is a complementary organism represented by the archetypal pair of yin and yang, which form the basis for ancient Chinese thought. The yin is the soft, feminine, receptive, earthly aspect of reality. The yang is the hard, masculine, active, heavenly aspect of reality. In Taoist wisdom both yin and yang are the complementary nature of the intuition and intellect. Both our intellect and intuition exist as an interplay of opposites within our consciousness. If we overcompensate and favor one over the other then we will have psychological imbalance. Our current society and culture reflects this imbalance as we continue to emphasize the yang aspect of reality. We are almost all in a process of "doing" something to "go" somewhere in the future. There is only a minority of people who are "nondoing" to get to the destination of here and now. Both are missing the point. In Taoism, the "Way," or Tao, can only be known through one's experience of the interplay of the yin and yang opposites. That is why in the Tao Te Ching Lao-tzu states:

> *Know the male,*
> *yet keep to the female:*
> *receive the world in your arms.*
> *If you receive the world,*
> *the Tao will never leave you*
> *and you will be like a little child.*[1]

This means to be content with your life, to trust and accept life within that yin stillness. And when the yang action is required, it will be a spontaneous movement out of the soft yin stillness. Both depend on each other for balance, and it is with this balance that we perceive Tao in the center of the circle that is half yin and half yang. It is an interplay of opposites that are intrinsically unified. This is the way things are with the intellect and intuition also. We cannot know anything deeply without the experience of life happening to us. The intellect has to read the maps before the intuition can unveil the meaning.

Patañjali expressed this opinion also. He emphasized that the effortlessness of enlightenment could not be known without some effort to achieve it. Patañjali devised a system of yoga—original yoga—focused on a practice of nondoing that gives birth to this effortlessness in active life.

The practice of Zen corresponds to Patañjali's view, as Zen teaches that within the tension of practice a lotus flower blooms. This flower represents the perception of enlightenment. In following the example of all these wisdom traditions and enlightened masters, we cannot have enlightenment for free without some effort to recognize this original nature within ourselves. Being to just *be* without any psychological or physical engagement with life is shortsighted. And on the other extreme, if we are just taught to practice to hopefully become enlightened one day, then this again is shortsighted, as one has no time for silence because one is always moving externally and internally.

Doing and nondoing go together, effort and effortlessness go together, the Middle Way of the Buddha is balance. Hold firm to effortlessness and do not ignore the time when some effort is needed. The intellectual intuition of esotericism is exactly this awareness. We realize in sincere self-work that the intellect is an instrument for decoding the experience of time, while intuition grows out of the void in the aspect of divine insight. Intellect is an instrument of time, and intuition is the voice and ear of the eternal. Both are complementary aspects of a human being's consciousness in relation to time and eternity. If they are complementary, time and eternity must also be complementary opposites. Our journey in time and our eternal destination, two opposites that most spiritual traditions divide their philosophies over, arise mutually and complement each other in the same way that we could not have the universe without yin and yang.

MUTUAL ARISING

The journey and the destination—one or the other of which one fixes one's spiritual focus on—are not different in any way. The function of the unified opposites of yin and yang is not one above the other and one is not more powerful than the other. They both mutually arise. Mutual arising is a key principle in Taoist wisdom, known in Chinese as *hsiang sheng* (相生). Hsiang sheng can unravel the riddle of our linear perspective of resonating with either a journey or destination. Mutual arising is a nonlinear awareness that conflicts with a definite reality of time.

The principle of hsiang sheng is perceived within all life. From the mysterious moment that the manifest world came into being, we see that the universe produced our consciousness, and our consciousness evoked the universe. From the yin and yang to the female and male human being, we discover that both unified complementary opposites arise mutually and are facilitators of harmony. Without both a male and a female our existence on this planet would be doomed. Likewise, we cannot have the intellect without intuition, as they naturally arise mutually. To fixate on one over the other puts our being out of balance with the way the universe is.

We seek to cultivate enlightenment through an arduous journey, or we try to discard everything so we can be at the destination right here and now: both approaches are faulty, according to the universal principle of mutual arising, or hsiang sheng. And this is why we see a lot of imbalance in those who seek enlightenment through only one modality. The imbalances are easy to perceive from a distance. For example, people who try to resonate with the destination and attempt to always "be here now" are lacking in intellect and so are easily swayed by others in time-bound matters. Likewise, those who are highly disciplined in practice in their constant effort to arrive at the destination of enlightenment are deaf to the divine voice of intuition. If we place one method above the other then enlightenment will remain as a phenomenon that is only read about in myth. This happens because we are either busy "doing" in order to get somewhere, or attempting to remain in "nondoing," which is usually flawed because we force ourselves to "be" without letting our nondoing arise naturally.

We discount the mutuality of doing and nondoing. In the same way that the universe produces consciousness and consciousness evokes the universe, nondoing produces doing and doing evokes nondoing. To make this more clear, being in the now is the only reality, as eternity exists in the present. But to realize this we must put forth at least some effort toward practice in order to evoke a consciousness capable of remaining completely in the now. It is completely paradoxical, but eternity cannot be sensed without paradox because our language is limited, and the world of time is only a mask and not something we can categorically pin down. Such is the paradoxical nature of hsiang sheng.

Being in the now and practicing mutually arise. Practice refines our consciousness to such a subtle state that we realize we have only forgot we were already enlightened. But we could not have realized this divine amnesia without a practice of some sort. Problems with our practice come only when we cling to our method of practice, as this is a subtle attempt to postpone our liberation. This viewpoint is in direct relation to our journey and destination.

When we embark on our spiritual journey through life we continually postpone the destination, as we are clinging to the scenery on our path. We put the destination off until the doorway of our future death from this world. We essentially get lost on our journey, but the journey is necessary. The journey is comparable to practice because in the same way practice refines our consciousness. Our journey continues to make us more humble and unravel our tight conditioning so we can realize that we were hypnotized. This hypnosis can sink back into the mind if we lose sight of the destination through the distractions of the journey, which eclipse the destination. We become busy always doing to get somewhere and fail to realize that the destination is here and now.

On the other hand, being in the now of the destination totally discards the journey. To become a Buddha is not to become a "stone Buddha," like the many statues you see in monasteries around the world that just sit there and are not alive. A stone Buddha symbolizes many things, but one of its primary meanings is the stillness it represents in the calm sitting posture. This stillness is confused with just remaining physically still, in sitting meditation, for example. But this is not a representation of true stillness, as this discards the masculine movement of the universe. Remember, motion and stillness are complementary opposites. So the stone Buddha represents stillness in all aspects of life: stillness within motion, and stillness within being still. It is the stillness of the mind, the transparent and reflective mirror of consciousness. This is the true destination, because along the journey we are always home in our original stillness.

When we force ourselves just to be in this destination, then this is a purely intellectual exercise. The true destination of stillness has to arise naturally through a practice not concerned about reaching anywhere else but now. Our practice should be a way of grooving with the eternal now. There is no separation. The journey is the destination and the destination is the journey. They paradoxically arise as one. This is the way of nature, the way of the Tao.

THE WAY OF ETERNAL BECOMING

The Way, Tao, is the mutual arising of the unified opposites of the journey or process, and is the destination within our consciousness and nature. The constant flow of change is an intrinsic interplay of opposites within the unified ocean of stillness. The pattern of nature and consciousness is a unified cyclical process of life. Yin and yang arise mutually and are interdependent, which creates the flow of perpetual change within the fluctuations of Tao.

Heraclitus of Ephesus also held this viewpoint of the journey and the destination being one. He believed that the world was in perpetual change, but he saw it as "eternal becoming." His awareness of this eternal becoming was the realization that perceived opposites are actually unified. Everything we experience, every little second of experience, is eternal becoming in the immediate moment. This unity of opposites, as Heraclitus taught, was split when the Eleatic school began to assume that the divine energy of the universe—that is, Brahman, Tao, Allah, God, and so on—is above humans and all life.* This is an ancient monarchical view that arose in those Eleatic schools, which obviously led to the Cartesian split of mind and matter.

The way of eternal becoming was discarded for a more intellectual approach to consciousness and nature. Thus, the Cartesian split of mind and matter was designed to understand both as two separate phenomena. The process of nature was thought to be separate from consciousness. All things are divided and compartmentalized, according to this perspective. The process or journey of life is a work in progress according to this view. The destination is a future where our mind has completely dominated the material world, bending it to the will of our egotistical cravings. This is our current view of the world, which puts humanity out of balance with nature, as we teeter on the tightrope of slipping into a full ecological crisis. The current view of the Cartesian split between mind and matter is not one that is held by the ancient sages because that implies that our journey right now is imperfect and that our destination is perfection. The way of nature, or way of the Tao, is to understand that the unified journey and destination is a mirror of mind and matter in eternal becoming.

---

*The Eleatic School was a pre-Socratic school of philosophy founded by the Greek philosopher Parmenides in the fifth century BCE in the ancient town of Elea.

Our modern view of the mind arises from the Eleatic school, and perceives the mind as a strange phenomenon arising from the brain. Though this is vaguely half-true, it is not an in-depth explanation of the function of mind. In the accepted view, mind is dealt with as a mere "thing" that most of us should not be too concerned about. Our focus shifts to matter as a result, and mind is used as a tool rather than something we should understand.

Some new systems of science, though, believe that mind and matter are more intimately related than we once thought. The Santiago theory of cognition postulates that the process of knowing (cognition) is identical with the process of all levels of living systems in life. According to the discoveries of the Santiago theory, mind is not a "thing" but is a living process like any other in nature. Scientifically this shatters any notion that mind and matter, consciousness and nature could be separate. But this new theory in science is old news to the mystics. The inner world of mind is reflected in the function of the outer world.

A sage perceives mind as a process that is part of nature's process, as in the Santiago theory. The mind's process manifests through the human body and brain. Nature and mind work in unison as one process. All of our contributions to human civilization, whether chaotic or orderly, are processes of mind. Human civilization is simply our mind exposed in the open. And in exposing the process of mind within civilization, we discover that the majority of humanity focus only on the "doing" aspect of reality.

Everything and everyone in our world is busy doing something and going somewhere. The process of our mind is predominately focused on the doing aspect of a journey to a future destination. The mind's process has begun to move artificially and out of sync with nature. We have compensated only for motion without stillness. As a result we have created an artificial mechanical world built on controlling nature and our experiences. The function of our mind is lopsided because of this process, and we are both consciously and unconsciously destroying the planet as a result. Our social anxiety is a reflection of only being busy trying to get to a destination that we never arrive at because we do not see in our stressful mind that the destination is right here and now. Many people never take a lot of time just "being silent" and doing nothing because they erroneously believe nothing can be achieved that way. Yet the universe is born of stillness, and any action you wish to bring into manifestation cannot be harmonious if it didn't arise in the nothingness of your being.

If doing is not an extension of nondoing, then we have the divided world we live in now because the individual is divided within. The accepted ideology that mind and matter are separate builds a schism within the psyche that contorts the natural function of mind.

THE UNITY OF DOING AND NONDOING

The natural function of mind is a process of life that is part of nature's unfolding. To understand the unity of doing and nondoing we need to look into the most subtle, humble, and transparent element in nature, water. Mind is a reflection of the subtlety of water. The process of water in nature is always moved by external vibrations that disturb its tranquility. When we see water move from the solid world of form—ice at the source of the Ganges River in the Himalayas, for example—it goes on a tremendous journey along a mountain stream and river until it gets to the great ocean. On this journey the water becomes turbulent at times when it is moved by external stimuli. But when the water is perfectly still, it is calm, transparent, and reflective. Paradoxically, though, when the water is in motion it's going to the great ocean while nourishing life along the way. Water can only move and nourish life in such a way because its motion arises from stillness and eventually goes back to stillness, without losing any of its purity no matter how polluted it becomes along the way. It is always in its original nature, and even when external factors disturb it, water will always go back to stillness.

The process of mind is exactly the same as this description of water. When mind activity is stimulated by external factors it begins to move in the process of nature. But if our original stillness of mind has been lost in this process, our activity of mind will not be nourishing life, or more correctly, will not be divinely inspired. As water represents mutual stillness and motion, our mind does too. The way of eternal becoming is to realize that mind is a process of nature and that both are essentially one. Without mind there is no matter, and without matter there is no mind. Both are intimately interwoven, but we confuse them as isolated opposites.

As water seeks to be one with the ocean, we seek to be one with the great ocean of consciousness, Brahman. And even as water seeks the great ocean, it is always one with the ocean along its journey, as it can never depart from its nature as water. So, too, are we one with the irreducible essence, even though we may be lost on a journey seeking it as if it were something separate. Furthermore, ice has the same essence as the water in the ocean, that is, it is unified. We are also unified with the great void. We are already one with that great ocean of the void, but we have forgotten that we are. As water comes from the heavens of the sky, we come from the stillness of the void, and can return any time we recognize that the eternal reality is now.

If the ice is the ocean, then a flowing river is the mirage of change that eclipses their unity. Likewise, with a human, the interplay of opposites that develops throughout the time and change of a journey eclipses our true destination of enlightenment here and now. Eternity and time, nirvana and samsara, now and the journey are all inseparable. The eternal great void is now in the journey called your life. The split between mind and matter, nondoing and doing, nowness and practice, and the destination and journey are illusory aspects of the flow of change caused by the yin and yang energies that ripple the clarity of the ocean's surface.

Eternity could not be anywhere else but right here and now in time, as the destination (nirvana) could not be anywhere else but in the journey (samsara). Enlightenment is the awareness of this unity within apparent duality created by the illusion of time. That jewel within the lotus flower of Buddhism and the Heart Sutra gives us a glimpse of the enlightenment that can only be ever-present in the apparent duality of the universe. The bodhisattva of compassion, Avalokitesvara, explains to Shariputra in the Heart Sutra:

> *Here, Shariputra,*
> *form is emptiness, emptiness is form;*
> *emptiness is not separate from form,*
> *form is not separate from emptiness;*
> *whatever is form is emptiness,*
> *whatever is emptiness is form.*[2]

10
Now Is Enlightenment

PERCEIVING UNITY within the illusion of duality ends the mental movement of time from past to future, instead leaving us only the present moment. The journey and the destination are mutually experienced in the eternity of here and now, where time and thinking cut out. When this is fully integrated into your being, life is forever fresh as the naturalness of spontaneity becomes conscious. Yet invariably only a sage can embody this eternal essence within the realm of the manifest.

It is increasingly difficult for the average individual to live completely in the present moment and act naturally spontaneous without any intention to do so. The majority of people living on this planet suffer from the anxiety and stress we accumulate from our society and culture, as we attempt to live up to the socially accepted models of success. In such a state of anxiety and stress it is almost impossible for the average individual to perceive unity within duality, because their suffering is a result of the belief in duality.

But it is not completely impossible; it is just more difficult for most of us than for a sage in isolation on a mountaintop. Chuang-tzu was one such sage who saw the benefit of remaining in society with his perception fixed on "the Tao of all things." His example proves that no matter what walk of life you are from, if your vision of reality has evolved, then the effortlessness you bring to life will be anywhere you choose to be, because it is not the result of any external influence. Rather, it has grown from within you to blossom its beauty and aroma into the world. It comes back to how sincere you are in your own self-work and introspection. Is your urge to be enlightened right now as important as your urge for money and prestige? Money and prestige always require excessive anxiety and stress to access.

Enlightenment, on the other hand, requires only that you know yourself beyond the constraints of time. We need to be mindful, though, that this is not easy for many people to realize. A good spiritual map is useful for the average person, until they realize they were already at the destination and so they no longer need the map.

Most good spiritual maps try to reveal the simplicity and naturalness at your core, because from that original place of beingness the awareness of unity is the fruit of enlightenment. But as I already mentioned, a sage is usually the only one who embodies this simple mind because many people are vexed by their propensity to always be active without rest or trust. This is why naturalness and spontaneity are thought of as difficult states of consciousness to cultivate. We cannot get out of our journey to a destination by "doing" mentality. Austrian-born American physicist Fritjof Capra emphasizes this in *The Tao of Physics* in relation to Zen Buddhism:

> The perfection of Zen is thus to live one's everyday life naturally and spontaneously. When Po-chang was asked to define Zen, he said, "When hungry eat, when tired sleep." Although this sounds simple and obvious, like so much in Zen, it is in fact quite a difficult task. To regain the naturalness of our original nature requires long training and constitutes a great spiritual achievement. In the words of a famous Zen saying,
>
> *Before you study Zen, mountains are mountains and rivers are rivers; while you are studying Zen, mountains are no longer mountains and rivers are no longer rivers; but once you have had enlightenment, mountains are once again mountains and rivers again rivers.*
>
> Zen's emphasis on naturalness and spontaneity certainly shows its Taoist roots, but the basis for this emphasis is strictly Buddhistic.

It is the belief in the perfection of our original nature, the realization that the process of enlightenment consists merely in becoming what we already are from the beginning.[1]

As we have discussed throughout this book, it is this "what we already are from the beginning" that is the hardest place to be within our consciousness. No matter how hard we try to remain in the now, our mind invariably comes back to distract us with thoughts attached to past or future.

In most cases, as Fritjof Capra explains, to be naturally spontaneous right now paradoxically requires some effort, or else the nowness we experience will be weak as it is mainly an intellectual exercise rather than an intuitive feeling. It is ridiculously paradoxical that we can never be anywhere else but now, yet to be consciously in the now we require a medicine for our ills. The medicine is the ancient art of meditation in its numerous forms. Meditation takes our awareness of nowness from theory to practice, and from doing to nondoing. Yet, as with most things in our world, meditation is treated as a tool to get "somewhere," which makes it purely intellectual and an instrument bound to time, neither natural nor eternal.

NOW IS REAL MEDITATION

Meditation is a spiritual practice that has been robbed of its original value over time. We find all sorts of meditative practices in our world, many of which are mainly centered on self-improvement rather than self-realization. Meditation has not escaped the "how will this benefit me" mentality of the world. The irony is that the only way a person improves or transforms is through realizing who they are deep within. This cannot be achieved through focusing on self-improvement, because all we are doing is improving our ego to be better in the eyes of others. Realizing your original nature does not improve your ego, but instead reduces its influence within your consciousness.

The habits, tendencies, and identification with conditioned belief systems all begin to reduce if we are seeking our original nature. Meditation is a practice to rediscover this original nature and it has nothing to do with you becoming more successful than others. The majority of meditation practices have veered away from their original forms and are more focused on exploring the limits of the mind.

Common practices of meditation in our world today are concerned with techniques using images, counting breaths, and focusing the mind on world peace or something else we want to happen in life. Though there is nothing inherently wrong with these methods, none of them are real meditation, because real meditation is within the silence beyond the realm of thought. The use of images in meditation, for example, is still in the field of thought. To focus on an image is to think about it. We cannot escape this because the very use of an image is from the field of mental concepts. Mental concepts are built on a time-bound framework. These sorts of practices, especially in ancient times, are more focused on magic and creating our own reality. Using images is thought to induce certain mental states, or bring about magic that is missing from our lives. But this approach is shortsighted because life itself is magical without our effort to make it so. The use of personal magic is a time-bound philosophy, as we yearn to create for the future and long for the "good times" of the past.

Meditation is a connection to eternity and has nothing to do with time. It is therefore magical. Using images to center our attention may be effective to a degree, but this is not real meditation. Some people who meditate on images, or practice other methods of thinking, have amazing experiences within their mind that are similar to psychedelic experiences. But again, this is not true meditation, because it is still in the realm of thought, as one is having an experience of "something."

Imagery is always a mental concept keeping us fixed to a time or place other than here and now. No image, not even the concept of God, can conjure up a state of real meditation. The image of God is used as a meditative tool by some religions. Yet, even though the image of God differs between most religions, to try and describe an image of mind is still within the process of thinking; it is not meditation and most surely not God. To use any image, symbol, and so on, is to completely miss the point of meditation. Real meditation is to perceive the nature of your mind and reality devoid of images, concepts, symbols, and so on. Devoid of all "things" and "thoughts," it is truly spiritual.

Real meditation is about nothing at all—not one thing, but actually "no thing." Sincere meditative practice stops the ripples of our excessive thinking in our mind and brings us face to face with the pure silence of the void, which is beyond name, form, or image. It is an experience of nothing, and one where you gain nothing. All that happens is that the flow of the stream of thoughts momentarily ceases, and nothing else. It is nondoing in the true sense of the word. Real meditation is not as glamorous as its cheap imitations.

This is why many people shy away from real meditation, because it is an experience of stillness that is out of accord with humanity's addiction to being active both within and without. Many people, including the spiritually inclined, can feel agitated at the thought of stillness. Yet real meditation is about an encounter with stillness, so it is imperative that we go beyond our agitation. When we dive into silence the agitated mind is understood. To understand anything comes from those moments when our mind is given the opportunity to rest, and out of that silent mind insights are born. In this sense, to continually silence the mind is to preserve intellectual life. Again, the nondoing and doing are mutual.

The naturalness of this mutuality cannot be controlled, yet paradoxically when we begin meditation practice, it is a medicine for hypnosis. But the "practice of meditation" is a placebo, because when we refine our consciousness with meditative practice we realize that real meditation is natural with no need of effort. When we are new to meditation, we take our placebo to try to control our practice. As a result we discover that meditation, like everything else, cannot be controlled because it is natural to the human organism.

The silence of our mind is natural; it is the center of our being, which is that aspect of our mind that corresponds to the mystery of the universe, because silence itself is mysterious. The more our mind is silent, the stronger our relationship to the mystery. Having a relationship with that mystery, that irreducible essence, our meditation becomes natural in life where mindfulness is the axis of our daily life. We don't get lost in the stories of thoughts in our mind, as past and future begin to fade. Our concerns for past and future fade because the real meditative state of silence grounds our awareness in the now. Real meditation is in the now, as pure silence is beyond the parameters of thought, which are the realm of time. Real meditation attunes our consciousness to a state of perception that is fixated in the originality of now, eternity, where our thoughts and distractions of mind have disappeared, and in doing so the vision of the divinely unified illuminates our being.

THE VISION OF UNITY

Once the mind is clear, reality too is clear. The delusion of name and form disappears. The illusion of separation dissolves into a sense of unity within consciousness. This perception of the Divine is often mentioned by numerous religions. But their descriptions are shortsighted because they are bound to doctrine and to a "Being" ruling over humanity. Doctrines and deities are ultimately instruments of time and not of the eternity they profess. If we are here to perceive the eternal unity of all things, how could we use time-bound instruments? It is impossible to perceive the eternal within the manifest when we are bound by spiritual maps, so we need to go beyond them. Enlightenment can never be our state if we are not prepared to go to the "yonder shore" within our consciousness. We need to go beyond doctrines, belief systems, graven images and so on, as the truly Divine is nameless and formless, thus a mystery.

A consciousness at a higher level of attunement perceives divinity within apparent separation from a state of awareness comparable to natural real meditation. This vision of unity is not some vision of separate components, such as religions or nations, coming together for world peace. On the contrary, latent within all those apparently separate components is "the Tao of all things" to use Chuang-tzu's words. It is the complete understanding of the Vedic hymn "All is Brahman and I am That." This is a state of consciousness that has stepped out of the parameters of time and thus can see reality as it truly is for the first time.

Organized religion will never perceive the Brahman in all because it has a doctrine built on doing moral social good and seeking individual pleasures to the exclusion of the social bad and individual psychological pain. What we call Allah, God, Brahman, Tao, and so on, is not a one-sided, personal lord, as most erroneously believe. If you are more attuned to your inner landscape you will know that the Divine in all things only keeps balance and does not take sides, since God has no humanlike ego. As Lao-tzu most wisely explains to humanity in the Tao Te Ching:

> *The great Tao flows everywhere,*
> *to the left and to the right.*
> *All things depend upon it to exist,*
> *and it does not abandon them.*
> *To its accomplishments it lays no claim.*
> *It loves and nourishes all things,*
> *but does not lord it over them.*[2]

The perception of the Divine, or Tao in Lao-tzu's words, in reality is to see through the eyes of God. The vision of the divine unity is not a perception where you see a deity or a personal God. On the contrary, it is a state of consciousness so still and pure that what you perceive is like looking in a mirror of your own inner being. The principle polarities of the universe, yin and yang, merge as one in this vision because in essence they are one. When both "this" and "that" are perceived in their dynamic unity, the "Way" or Tao of the universe, which is the natural spontaneity of life in the now, is lived as a vivid reality. A sage imbibes this state of consciousness, and so too can we, as "the way that cannot be told" is our original nature. Living in this original nature, a sage brings harmony to the world not by trying to do so, but because her consciousness is naturally harmonious. The great Taoist sage Chuang-tzu expresses this point in the most humorously profound way:

> To use an attribute to show that attributes are not attributes is not as good as using a non-attribute to show that attributes are not attributes. To use a horse to show that a horse is not a horse is not as good as using a non-horse to show that a horse is not a horse, Heaven and earth are one attribute; the ten thousand things are one horse. . . .
>
> . . . Whether you point to a little stalk or a great pillar, a leper or the beautiful Hsi-shih, things ribald and shady or things grotesque and strange, the Way makes them all into one. Their dividedness is their completeness; their completeness is their impairment. No thing is either complete or impaired, but all are made into one again. Only the man of far-reaching vision knows how to make them into one. So he has no use [for categories], but relegates all to the constant. The constant is the useful; the useful is the passable; the passable is the successful; and with success, all is accomplished. He relies upon this alone, relies upon it and does not know he is doing so. This is called the Way.
>
> But to wear out your brain trying to make things into one without realizing that they are all the same—this is called "three in the morning." What do I mean by "three in the morning"? When the monkey trainer was handing out acorns, he said, "You get three in the morning and four at night." This made all the monkeys furious. "Well, then," he said, "you get four in the morning and three at night." The monkeys were all delighted. There was no change in

the reality behind the words, and yet the monkeys responded with joy and anger. Let them, if they want to. So the sage harmonizes with both right and wrong and rests in Heaven the Equalizer. This is called walking two roads.[3]

Walking two roads, a sage resides in that aeviternal place between the form and the formless, which is the Middle Way of the Buddha. As Chuang-tzu mysteriously points out, nothing of the physical reality changes except your deeper level of consciousness, which perceives reality on a deeper and subtler level. Separate forms still have their place, but your perception can sense the unity intuitively in all forms. This vision of unity is not a time-bound concept that we can seek actively in the future. The vision of unity is the irreducible essence of the universe that we know to be eternal. So to have this evolved perception of the vision of unity can only be a conscious experience in the now and nowhere else, because right here and now is where thoughts and thinking cut out to reveal the eternity hiding in front of our face. Usually, when someone has this experience it is in quiet contemplation and meditation because the active mind has ceased and a stilling of the mind, known as *nirodha* in Sanskrit, has taken place.

Real meditation, which is empty stillness and silence, evokes the vision of unity, as it is a way of dancing with the nowness of eternity. And paradoxically, the vision of unity evokes stillness within the mind. The stillness of mind evokes the vision of God in all, and vice versa. This is a state of consciousness in which time and eternity, samsara and nirvana, are recognized as ultimately one. The Shiva Nataraja, the image of the Hindu god Shiva as Lord of the Dance, conceals the cosmic dance of unity between the rhythm and vibration of time and eternity. Shiva destroys the deluded mind to bring the breath of Brahma back into the stillness of consciousness through the dance of Shiva (see figure 10.1 on page 150).

As the Shiva Nataraja conceals the truth of the unity within the rhythm and vibration of opposites, so do we conceal that truth with

Figure 10.1. Shiva Nataraja

our beliefs, concepts, images, and anything else that colors our pure consciousness. Moving away from the distractions of time, we find ourselves in the stillness of now, where the peace you are is the peace you give to the world.

ENLIGHTENMENT NEVER LEFT YOU

Collective peace and harmony in our world depends on our ability to bring that concealed truth forth individually, which is the enlightenment we already are right now, beyond the illusion of the veils and seals of time. Our yearning for future accomplishments, nostalgia, and disappointments of the past keep us away from the reality of the now and our original nature. The illusion of past and future deludes our mind from staying in the present moment. This delusion maintains our focus on building an identity in the future that is based on what we have experienced in the past. Though we are all guilty of the need to improve society and searching for self-improvement of our identity, both eclipse our original and authentic self right now.

This propensity to improve ourselves and society is always based on the instruments of time, beliefs, concepts, and so on. We all impose our will upon another, in either subtle or obvious ways, just so we can condition other people with our own conditioning in order to make our life more pleasurable through the denial of pain.

To use an obvious example of this tendency toward "improvement," think of the Europeans traveling the world in ancient times, preaching and indoctrinating indigenous cultures into Christianity. These cultures were perfectly fine before the Europeans arrived. The problems and confusion within indigenous cultures were exacerbated when the Europeans came and interfered with their natural way of life, which ultimately ruined the grounded spiritual shamanism of many indigenous cultures. Those fooled by the past and future tend to impose their will over others because there is no awareness that reality is right now and nowhere else.

All wars, and our contempt for nature, are spawned from this attempt to build our identity and world based on the thoughts of past and future. The control we seek on the individual level becomes the destruction we experience on the collective level. The wars and discord of our world are the result of this control system, which is based on the thinker of thoughts. To let go of control is to come back into the present, where the knots of the heart are untied. The Jamaican spiritual teacher Mooji beautifully said:

> The doer of actions and the thinker of thoughts is causing all the trouble in the world. That identity. And it is false, it's not true. The vital force itself is the animating power of this universe. The human being is itself an effect in consciousness, it is not the operator or controller of consciousness. If one understands this, a great unburdening takes place.[4]

Your identity, which is built by time, is not who you truly are in the eternal realm. In actuality, your clinging to identity only gets in the way of your enlightenment now. The identity itself is innocent. It is our *belief* in the identity that starts trouble. We suffer from the catastrophe of being unable to step outside our time-bound identity. The distractions of past and future sustain our belief in this identity in time. Hypnotized, we forget who we truly are right now. To be doing "this" and "that" is fine, but to forget the real you behind the mask of identity is the true tragedy. Your identity is not enlightened, but the real you is. Beyond name, beyond form, is the ground of your being, not the mask of the actor in this play.

When we stray away from the now we forget our original enlightened nature. Our addiction to time and thoughts eclipses the ultimate reality of who we truly are. Time veils the mystery of eternity for most of us. But eternity is always there right now, beyond our awareness of it. Enlightenment is lived through complete dehypnotization because hypnosis is the result of mental activity moved by time and our belief in time. The thoughts of past and future induce an artificial form of amnesia, so that we forget who we truly are.

This amnesia, resulting from excessive thoughts and thinking, is like trying to remember someone's name, but we can't quite remember it even though it is on the tip of our tongue. No matter how hard we concentrate we cannot remember their name. It is only when we give up our search and our attention shifts to something else that we suddenly remember it. In the process of giving up our search, as Gautama the Buddha did under the Bodhi tree, no thinking is involved, and as a result, a sudden immediate insight comes to the mind. The spontaneity of naturalness comes into existence when there is no thinking about whatever it may be. By "thinking about it" I mean searching for it as if it is a state of consciousness acquired in time. In the same way that we remember someone's name after we stop thinking about it, we also remember that we are enlightened when we stop thinking about enlightenment.

To search for enlightenment is to postpone it, as the Buddha realized. Searching for something that we already have is useless. The great Zen master Po-chang was asked about seeking our Buddha nature (that is, our original nature, or enlightenment). Po-chang answered, "It's much like riding an ox in search of the ox."[5]

As with the ox, enlightenment has never departed from our consciousness. To search for it is to delay its reality right here and now. *Now* is all that exists, and your enlightenment is the anchor of eternity within time, illuminating the ignorance and suffering of our world, which are under the spell of time. In this illumination there is nowhere else to be but to read these very words that your eyes perceive. So simple and humble, just resting right here with no anxiety for past or future. This right now is your enlightened nature and you are That. *Tat tvam asi:* you are That right now, and the real you has never been anything or anywhere else.

Notes

INTRODUCTION. OUT OF TIME AND INTO ENLIGHTENMENT

1. Ramacharaka, *Lessons in Gnani Yoga,* 11–12.
2. Patañjali, *Yoga-Sūtra*, 2.
3. Watts, *Way of Zen*, 78–79.
4. Huxley, *Perennial Philosophy,* 299.

1. MONARCHICAL VIEW OF THE UNIVERSE

1. Three Initiates, *Kybalion,* 38.
2. Society of Archbishop Justus, *The Book of Common Prayer,* http://justus
   .anglican.org/resources/bcp/Shorter/preay&thanks.htm.
3. Campbell, *Myths of Light,* xvi.

2. A SUPERFICIAL INITIATION INTO THE FUTURE

1. Chuang Tzu, *Complete Works*, 5–6.
2. Masters, *Spiritual Bypassing,* 1–2.
3. Holman, *Return of the Perennial Philosophy,* 13.
4. Patañjali, *Yoga-Sūtra*, xii–xii, 3, 12–13.
5. Blake, *Complete Poetry and Prose*, 490.
6. Kingsley, *Reality,* 102–3.

3. THE OCCULT INITIATION OF PURUSHA
(PURE AWARENESS)

1. Holman, *Return of the Perennial Philosophy,* 47.
2. Three Initiates, *Kybalion,* 26, 28, 30.
3. Ibid., 26–27.
4. Ibid., 35.
5. Campbell, *Myths of Light,* 29–30.
6. Swami Satchidananda, goodreads.com.

4. THE IMPERFECTION AND NONEVENT
OF ENLIGHTENMENT

1. Carlin, *Jammin' in New York.*
2. Dyer, *Wisdom of the Ages,* 35.
3. Lao Tzu, *Tao Te Ching,* chapter 2.
4. Patañjali, *Yoga-Sūtra,* xv–xvi.
5. Yukteswar, *Holy Science,* 102.
6. Ibid., 102, 75.

5. FAST-FOOD SPIRITUAL JUNKIE

1. Ouspensky, *In Search of the Miraculous,* 144.
2. Lao Tzu, *Tao Te Ching,* chapter 1.
3. Masters, *Spiritual Bypassing,* 160–62.
4. Watts, *Way of Zen,* 127–28.
5. Watts, *Wisdom of Insecurity,* 20–22.
6. Wikiquote.org, *Fight Club* (Film) http://en.wikiquote.org/wiki/Fight_Club_(film).

7. ENLIGHTENED ATTUNEMENT

1. Werner Heisenberg, quoted in http://en.wikiquote.org/wiki/Werner_Heisenberg.
2. Alfred Korzybski, quoted in http://en.wikipedia.org/wiki/The_map_is_not_the_territory.
3. Campbell, *Myths of Light,* xvii–xviii.

4. Talbot, *Holographic Universe,* 174–76.
5. Gregory, *Science and Practice of Humility,* 97–98.

8. THE PATTERN AND ORDER OF UNIVERSAL CONSCIOUSNESS

1. Chuang Tsu, *Chuang Tsu: Inner Chapters,* 29.
2. Wilhelm, *Secret of the Golden Flower,* 91.
3. Wilhelm, *I Ching,* 78.
4. Griffith, *Hymns of the Rgveda,* 246.
5. Fix, *Pyramid Odyssey,* 126.

9. THE JOURNEY IS THE DESTINATION AND THE DESTINATION IS THE JOURNEY

1. Lao Tzu, *Tao Te Ching,* chapter 28.
2. Red Pine, *Heart Sutra,* 2.

10. NOW IS ENLIGHTENMENT

1. Fritjof Capra, *Tao of Physics,* 124.
2. Watts, *Way of Zen,* 18.
3. Chuang Tzu, *Complete Works,* 40–41.
4. Mooji.org, *You Know It's a Movie—Mooji,* www.youtube.com/watch?v=LGJy8VrU-Ec.
5. Capra, *Tao of Physics,* 124.

Bibliography

Benoit, Hubert. *Zen and the Psychology of Transformation*. Rochester, Vt.: Inner Traditions, 1990.

Blake, William. *The Complete Poetry and Prose of William Blake*. Oakland, Calif.: University of California Press, 2008.

Blofeld, John. *Taoism: Road to Immortality*. Boston, Mass.: Shambhala, 2000.

Campbell, Joseph. *Myths of Light*. Novato, Calif.: New World Library, 2003.

Capra, Fritjof. *The Tao of Physics*. Boston, Mass.: Shambhala, 2000.

Chuang Tsu. *Chuang Tsu: Inner Chapters, A Companion Volume to Tao Te Ching*. Translated by Gia-Fu Feng and Jane English. Portland, Ore.: Amber Lotus, 2008.

———. *The Complete Works of Chuang Tzu*. Translated by Burton Watson. New York: Columbia University Press, 1968.

Cleary, Thomas. *The Taoism Reader*. Boston, Mass.: Shambhala, 2012.

Dyer, Wayne W. *Wisdom of the Ages: 60 Days to Enlightenment*. New York: William Morrow, 2002.

Easwaran, Eknath, trans. *The Upanishads*. Tomales, Calif.: Nilgiri Press, 2007.

Fix, William R. *Pyramid Odyssey*. Urbanna, Va.: Mercury Media, Inc., 1984.

Gregory, Jason. *The Science and Practice of Humility*. Rochester, Vt.: Inner Traditions, 2014.

Griffith, Ralph T. H. *The Hymns of the Rgveda*. Delhi, India: Motilal Banarsidass Publishers, 1999.

Holman, John. *The Return of the Perennial Philosophy*. London: Watkins, 2008.

Huxley, Aldous. *The Perennial Philosophy*. New York: Harper Perennial Modern Classics, 2009.

Kingsley, Peter. *Reality*. Point Reyes, Calif.: The Golden Sufi Center, 2004.

Krishnamurti, Jiddu. *Krishnamurti: Reflections on the Self*. Chicago, Ill.: Open Court, 1998.

———. *Total Freedom*. New York: Harper One, 1996.

Lao-tzu. *Tao Te Ching: An Illustrated Journey*. Translated by Stephen Mitchell. London: Frances Lincoln, 2009.

Maharshi, Sri Ramana. *Saddarsanam and An Inquiry into the Revelation of Truth and Oneself*. Translated by Nome. Santa Cruz, Calif: Society of Abidance in Truth, 2009.

Masters, Robert Augustus. *Spiritual Bypassing*. Berkeley, Calif.: North Atlantic Books, 2010.

Merton, Thomas. *The Way of Chuang Tzu*. New York: New Directions, 2010.

Naimy, Mikhail. *The Book of Mirdad*. London: Watkins, 1999.

Ouspensky, P. D. *In Search of the Miraculous: The Teachings of G. I. Gurdjieff*. Orlando, Fla.: Harcourt, 2001.

Patañjali. *The Yoga-Sūtra of Patañjali*. Translated and commentary by Chip Hartranft. Boston, Mass.: Shambhala, 2003.

Pine, Red. *The Heart Sutra*. Berkeley, Calif.: Counterpoint, 2005.

Ramacharaka, Yogi. *Advance Course in Yogi Philosophy and Oriental Occultism*. Chicago, Ill.: The Yogi Publication Society, 1931.

———. *Fourteen Lessons in Yogi Philosophy and Oriental Occultism*. Chicago, Ill.: The Yogi Publication Society, 1931.

———. *Lessons in Gnani Yoga*. Chicago, Ill.: The Yogi Publication Society, 1934.

Schuon, Frithjof. *The Transcendent Unity of Religions*. Wheaton, Ill.: Quest Books, 1984.

Suzuki, Daisetz Teitaro, trans. *The Lankavatara Sutra: A Mahayana Text*. Philadelphia, Pa.: Coronet Books, 1999.

Suzuki, Shunryu. *Zen Mind, Beginner's Mind*. Boston, Mass.: Shambhala, 2011.

Talbot, Michael. *The Holographic Universe*. New York: HarperCollins, 1996.

Three Initiates. *The Kybalion: Hermetic Philosophy*. Chicago, Ill.: The Yogi Publication Society, 1940.

Watts, Alan. *Do You Do It, or Does It Do You: How to Let the Universe Meditate You.* Audio CD. Louisville, Colo.: Sounds True, 2005.

———. *Out of Your Mind: Essential Listening from the Alan Watts Audio Archives.* Audio CD. Louisville, Colo.: Sounds True, 2004.

———. *Tao: The Watercourse Way.* New York: Pantheon, 1977.

———. *The Way of Zen.* New York: Vintage Books, 1999.

———. *The Wisdom of Insecurity.* New York: Vintage Books, 2011.

Welwood, John. *Perfect Love, Imperfect Relationships.* Boston, Mass.: Trumpeter, 2007.

———. *Toward a Psychology of Awakening.* Boston, Mass.: Shambhala, 2002.

Wilhelm, Richard. *The I Ching or Book of Changes.* Princeton, N.J.: Princeton University Press, 1967.

———. *The Secret of the Golden Flower: A Chinese Book of Life.* London: Arkana, 1984.

Yukteswar, Swami Sri. *The Holy Science.* Los Angeles: Self-Realization Fellowship, 1990.

Index

Numbers in *italics* indicate illustrations.